IS ANYONE
RESPONSIBLE?

American Politics and Political Economy Series
Edited by Benjamin I. Page

IS ANYONE RESPONSIBLE?

HOW TELEVISION FRAMES POLITICAL ISSUES

SHANTO IYENGAR

The University of Chicago Press
Chicago and London

Shanto Iyengar, professor of political science and communication studies at the University of California, Los Angeles, is coauthor, with Donald R. Kinder, of *News That Matters: Television and American Opinion* (University of Chicago Press, 1987).

The University of Chicago Press, Chicago 60637
The University of Chicago Press, Ltd., London
© 1991 by The University of Chicago
All rights reserved. Published 1991
Printed in the United States of America

00 99 98 97 96 95 94 93 92 91   5 4 3 2 1

Library of Congress Cataloging-in-Publication Data

Iyengar, Shanto.
    Is anyone responsible? : how television frames political issues /
Shanto Iyengar.
        p.   cm. — (American politics and political economy series)
    Includes bibliographical references and index.
    1. Television broadcasting of news—Political aspects—United
States.   2. Television broadcasting of news—Social aspects—United
States.   3. Television and politics—United States.   4. Journalism—
Objectivity—Public opinion.   I. Title.   II. Series: American
politics and political economy.
    PN4888.T4I93   1991
    302.23′45—dc20   91-13714
                                                                          CIP

ISBN: 0226-38854-9 (cloth)

Contents

Contents

Acknowledgments

This research could not have been carried out without the support and assistance of several individuals and institutions. I am indebted to several student assistants (both graduate and undergraduate) at the State University of New York at Stony Brook and at the University of California, Los Angeles who participated in the various phases of this study. Sholeh Khorooshi was indispensable to the project. She compiled and "created" all the experimental manipulations and coordinated the day-to-day scheduling of the experiments. Kimberly Heilig, Silvo Lenart, and Kenrick Leung were expert and reliable coders. Adam Behar, Tony Bloome, James Lo, and Adam Simon painstakingly combed the Vanderbilt *Abstracts* in search of network news stories. Kee Park and Jeff Tanenbaum at Stony Brook and Pradeep Chibber at UCLA provided critical data-related assistance. Adam Simon converted ponderous tables into sleek graphs.

Financial backing for the experiments was provided by a grant from the Political Science Program at the National Science Foundation (SES84-20160). Additional support was provided by Academic Senate grants from the University of California. A generous grant from the John and Mary R. Markle Foundation enabled me to reduce my teaching load and thus complete the manuscript on schedule.

Several colleagues and friends were kind enough to read and respond to papers that developed the arguments and analyses presented in this work. Kathleen McGraw and Robert S. Wyer, Jr. directed me to relevant work in cognitive and social psychology. Thomas Schwartz helped me recognize instances of framing in the economics literature. Benjamin Page and Samuel Popkin offered substantial critical feedback on earlier versions of the manuscript. Stephen Ansolabehere and George Tsebelis provided guidance on issues of significance. Ellen Robb's extensive revisions strengthened the manuscript both intellectually and stylistically.

Finally, I thank my family—Ellen, Nikhil, and Ranjana—for intellectual, emotional, and motivational sustenance.

IS ANYONE
RESPONSIBLE?

Introduction

The latter half of the twentieth century may well go down as the age of television. Television takes up more of the typical American's waking hours than interpersonal interaction. Scholars from all of the behavioral sciences have been fascinated with the medium and have attributed a kaleidescope of effects—ranging from the stimulation of violence to the learning of altruism—to television viewing. A recent compilation of the social science literature identified no fewer than 1,043 effects (both antisocial and social) of television on social behavior.[1]

In the area of public affairs, the impact of television has been widely condemned. As the dominant form of mass communication, television is said to have contributed to a variety of maladies including reduced voter turnout, discounting of substantive issues in political campaigns, decline of the political parties, automatic reelection of incumbents, increased use of rhetorical and symbolic rather than problem-solving strategies of leadership and governance, and other fundamental changes in the political system.[2] The unprecedented public popularity and significant policy successes of President Reagan, for instance, have been widely attributed to his mastery of television.[3]

Many claims regarding television's impact on the political process rest on less than robust evidence, however. In some instances, disentangling the influence of television from that of alternative causal forces has proven impossible. Moreover, some of the claims are contradictory. For example, those who regard television news as essentially "adversarial" have suggested that television breeds public cynicism toward government, while others, who regard television news as basically "deferential," have argued that television plays into the hands of the political establishment.

The only area of political life in which the impact of television has been empirically established is public opinion. For most Americans, the world of public affairs exists primarily in the *son et lumière* of television news shows. As the public's "mind's eye," television effectively sets the political agenda; the themes and issues that are repeated in television news coverage become the priorities of viewers.[4] Issues and events highlighted by television news become especially influential as criteria for evaluating public officials and choosing between political candidates.[5] There is also evidence that television news persuades viewers to alter their opinions; when the content of news stories is tiled in favor of particular policies or programs, public support for them increases.[6]

This work extends the analysis of television's impact on public opinion to the important questions of political responsibility and accountability. Specifically, the present research explores the direct impact of "episodic" and "thematic" news formats, or "frames," on viewers' attributions of responsibility for political issues and the indirect effects of these frames on public opinion in general. The premise of this research is that news about political issues almost invariably takes either an episodic or thematic frame. The episodic news frame focuses on specific events or particular cases, while the thematic news frame places political issues and events in some general context.

It is well known that television news is distinctively episodic in its depiction of political issues.[7] During the 1980s, for instance, network newscasts showed hundreds of reports of particular acts of terrorism but virtually no reports on the socioeconomic or political antecedents of terrorism.[8] The corollary of television's reliance on episodic framing is that issues that cannot be readily reduced to the level of specific events or occurrences, such as global warming, are seldom covered at all.[9]

The predominance of episodic framing in television news affects not only the networks' selection of news items, but also the public's attributions of responsibility for political issues. In particular, the studies reported here demonstrate that exposure to episodic news makes viewers less likely to hold public officials accountable for the existence of some problem and also less likely to hold them responsible for alleviating it. By discouraging viewers from attributing responsibility for national issues to political actors, television decreases the public's control over their elected representatives and the policies they pursue.

The basic constructs of attribution of responsibility and news frames are outlined in chapters 1 and 2. The essential argument is that attribution of responsibility—which is critical to the exercise of civic control—is very much a function of how television news frames the issues. By presenting the news in either thematic or episodic form, television influences attributions of responsibility both for the creation of problems or situations (causal responsibility) and for the resolution of these problems or situations (treatment responsibility).

This research investigates framing effects using multiple research methods, including content analysis of network newscasts, field experiments, and correlational analysis of national surveys. Chapter 3 describes these methods.

Chapters 4 and 5 assess the extent of thematic and episodic framing in network news reports broadcast between 1981 and 1986 dealing with the issues of crime, international terrorism, poverty, unemployment, and racial inequality. News coverage of poverty, crime, and terrorism was predominantly episodic; coverage of racial inequality tended to feature both episodic and thematic reports; and coverage of unemployment was primarily thematic. These chapters then describe several experiments that tested the impact of network framing on attributions of causal and treatment responsibility. With the exception of unemployment, attribution of responsibility was sensitive to whether the news reports framed the issue episodically or thematically; while thematic reports increased attributions of responsibility to government and society, episodic reports had the opposite effect. In addition to the distinction between episodic and thematic framing, other facets of the news were also found to affect attributions of responsibility. In the case of poverty, for example, news reports about a black poor person tended to elicit more individualistic attributions of responsibility than reports on a white poor person. Similarly, compared with news coverage of criminal acts carried out by blacks, news stories depicting white perpetrators elicited more frequent societal attributions of responsibility for crime.

Chapter 6 shifts the focus to the Iran-Contra affair. Here the news coverage was analyzed in terms of subject matter rather than stylistic frames. Content analysis of all Iran-Contra stories broadcast between

November 1986 and September 1987 revealed that this coverage could be characterized as oriented toward either the political or the policy implications of the affair. In other words, a distinction was drawn between news stories that focused on the domestic political controversy surrounding the arms sales and news stories that described the intended policy objectives of the Reagan administration. It was found that these alternative news frames influenced the extent to which viewers held President Reagan personally responsible for the decision. Specifically, presidential responsibility was heightened under conditions of political framing; political framing of the arms sale thus undermined President Reagan's popularity. Under conditions of policy framing, however, attributions of responsibility were less likely to focus on particular qualities of the president (e.g., Reagan's lack of knowledge) and more likely to focus on situational pressures (e.g., the war between Iran and Iraq).

Chapters 7 and 8 consider the question of whether attribution of responsibility is a relevant cue for political opinions and attitudes. In other words, the question is whether political opinions are affected by attributions of causal and treatment responsibility for issues. Chapter 7 demonstrates that attribution of responsibility is a powerful but issue-specific opinion cue: opinions on poverty are powerfully shaped by attributions of responsibility for poverty, opinions on terrorism are dictated by attributions of responsibility for terrorism, and so on. Chapter 8 indicates that in comparison with other long-standing influences such as party affiliation, the effects of attribution of responsibility on *general* political attitudes are less prominent.

Chapter 9 considers potential limitations on media framing effects. The first limitation concerns individual differences in susceptibility to framing. Some characteristics of the audience (such as political ideology and party identification) conditioned framing; others (including the viewer's level of education) had no significant effect. The second limitation concerns the degree to which network framing of a particular issue influences attributions of responsibility for related issues. Does episodic framing of *poverty*, for instance, influence attributions of responsibility for *racial inequality?* The evidence revealed little spillover in framing effects, even between closely related issues such as poverty and unemployment. For this sample of issues, framing effects were confined to specific issues.

The conclusion develops parallels between framing and other previously documented media effects on public opinion. A general psychological account of these effects as stemming from information accessibility is proposed. The political ramifications of framing, including the strategic value of television news for political elites and the effects of television on ideological reasoning, are identified. By portraying issues primarily as discrete events or instances, television news impedes recognition of the interconnections between issues and thus contributes to the absence of ideological constraint or consistency in American public opinion. In the same way, television's unswerving focus on specific episodes, individual perpetrators, victims, or other actors at the expense of more general, thematic information inhibits the attribution of political responsibility to societal factors and to the actions of politicians such as the president. These effects make elected officials and public institutions less accountable to the American public.

ONE

Why Responsibility Matters

For the ordinary American, the course of public affairs is very much "the mystery off there." Most Americans possess meager information about current issues and events, and virtually all political issues are beyond the range of personal experience. Low levels of citizen awareness do not preclude political opinionation, however; most Americans can and do express policy preferences on a wide range of political issues. The challenge of public opinion research has been to reconcile the low levels of personal relevance and visibility of most political issues with the plethora of issue opinions—policy preferences, evaluations of public officials, and the like—that large proportions of the population profess to hold. How do people manage to express opinions about such issues as civil rights legislation, economic assistance for the newly freed nations of Eastern Europe, or President Bush's performance at the international drug summit when these matters are so remote from matters of daily life and so few citizens are politically informed?

The conventional wisdom concerning the intelligibility of political issues holds that the public's opinions on specific issues are derived from either a "global" world view or "domain-specific" cues. The classic global view posits the existence of overarching, higher-order constructs, such as liberal or conservative ideology, political party affiliation, subjective utility, self-interest, and socioeconomic and cultural values. The global view hypothesizes that persons who can be classified as "liberal" or "conservative" are characterized by distinct opinion profiles on the entire range of public affairs issues. Most empirical tests of the global view have, however, uncovered only modest connections between issue-specific opinions and abstract universals.[1]

In response to the seeming lack of evidence for the global view, researchers have begun to turn to narrower and more idiosyncratic conceptualizations of political opinionation. The newer, "domain-specific" approaches hypothesize that opinions are based on narrower and more focused considerations relevant to particular issues.[2]

This work advances a domain-specific theory of public opinion in which the primary factor that determines opinions concerning political issues is the assignment of responsibility for the issue in question; that is, individuals tend to simplify political issues by reducing them to questions of responsibility, and their opinions on issues flow from their answers to these questions. Under this theory, the paramount task of public opinion research is to determine how people attribute responsibility for political issues.

Assigning Responsibility for National Issues

Attributions of responsibility are critical ingredients of all social knowledge. While acknowledging that responsibility may be assigned according to varied criteria, psychological research has focused on causality and treatment as particularly compelling definitions. "Causal responsibility" focuses on the origin of a problem, while "treatment responsibility" focuses on who or what has the power to alleviate (or forestall alleviation of) the problem.[3] Thus, if the problem of unemployment is assessed in terms of causal responsibility, the relevant questions concern the processes by which individuals lose or fail to obtain jobs. Treatment responsibility, on the other hand, seeks to establish who has the power (and interest) to alleviate or perpetuate unemployment.

These two definitions of responsibility are especially relevant for understanding political issues and events. Why certain problems occur and how they may be treated are recurring themes in political life. In the 1988 presidential campaign, for example, Americans were repeatedly asked to consider the locus of responsibility—both causal and treatment—for the federal budget deficit, crime, the Reagan administration's sale of arms to the government of Ayatollah Khomeini, and numerous other issues. Politicians also typically behave as though their political future depends upon their constituents' attributions of responsibility for public events: witness the alacrity with which they claim responsibility for favorable outcomes and deny or shirk responsibility for unfavorable outcomes.[4] By focusing public attention on the actions of Willie Horton (a convict who raped a woman while on a weekend furlough from a Massachusetts prison) and the state of Boston Harbor, President Bush's famous campaign advertisements effectively suggested that Governor Dukakis was a cause of crime and pollution, rather than an agent of treatment or control.

Popular culture also supplies political cues phrased in terms of responsibility. For example, the pervasive belief that poverty exists because poor people are lazy and that hard work is the best way out of financial adversity makes it possible to "know" that poor individuals are responsible for their situation. Limited factual expertise does not deter people from attributing responsibility for political issues.

There is ample evidence of the prominence of causal and treatment responsibility in everyday reasoning. Attributions of responsibility are made spontaneously and powerfully influence self-images, evaluations of other people, and emotional arousal.[5] Attributions of responsibility also exert a powerful hold on behavior, so much so that "misattribution" techniques have proven effective in treating behavior disorders, in inducing positive social behaviors, and even in extending longevity and strengthening general psychological well-being.[6] Responsibility is so compelling a concept that people even invent responsibility where none exists—as in purely random, or chance, events.[7]

More relevant to political reasoning, several scholars have demonstrated that attributions of responsibility for personal situations independently influence political attitudes. Individuals attributing responsibility for personal economic problems to themselves are significantly more approving of government than those attributing responsibility to society-at-large.[8] In addition, a vast literature on "retrospective" voting and the impact of economic conditions on election outcomes suggests that voters reward or punish incumbents at the polls according to the state of current or past national conditions.[9] One of the important implications of the evidence reported in this book is that television news weakens this "reward-punishment" electoral cycle by discouraging viewers from making societal attributions for issues.

In sum, there is substantial evidence, primarily in nonpolitical domains, to suggest that attributions of causal and treatment responsibility for national issues will dictate the opinions people hold on these issues. People think about responsibility instinctively, and attribution of responsibility represents a powerful psychological cue.

There are two distinct explanations of the process of attribution of issue responsibility. The first, which is a simple extension of the global view of public opinion, treats attribution as a product of stable, internal predispositions such as cultural values or political ideology. For example, in this view, conservatives will be more likely to consider victims responsible for social problems such as poverty or racial inequality, while liberals will be more likely to hold society or political actors responsible. According to this theory, how individuals assign responsibility is part and parcel of long-standing political predispositions.

While there can be no denying the influence of stable dispositional characteristics or cultural norms on attributions of responsibility for political issues, there is compelling evidence that contextual or circumstantial factors are equally—if not more—important. Just as individual behavior is marked by variability rather than consistency across situations, so too are attributions of responsibility likely to depend upon the context in which political issues and events appear.[10] Today, the most important of these contextual influences is television news.

TWO

Framing Effects of News Coverage

Converging evidence from several behavioral sciences indicates that people are exquisitely sensitive to contextual cues when they make decisions, formulate judgments, or express opinions. The manner in which a problem of choice is "framed" is a contextual cue that may profoundly influence decision outcomes. At the most general level, the concept of framing refers to subtle alterations in the statement or presentation of judgment and choice problems, and the term "framing effects" refers to changes in decision outcomes resulting from these alterations. Significant framing effects have been demonstrated in experimental studies of choice and in survey studies concerning the effects of question wording on response patterns. This chapter reviews the experimental and survey evidence concerning framing and develops a typology of news frames for analyzing television news as a contextual determinant of attributions of responsibility for political and social problems.

Framing: The Literature

The cognitive psychologists Daniel Kahneman and Amos Tversky have demonstrated in a series of experiments that choices between risky prospects can be powerfully altered merely by changing the terms in which equivalent choices are described.[1] When alternative outcomes are defined in terms of potential gains, people follow a risk-averting strategy, but when the equivalent outcomes are described in terms that suggest potential losses, people seek risk. In one of their experiments, Kahneman and Tversky posed the following question:

> Imagine that the U.S. is preparing for the outbreak of an unusual Asian disease, which is expected to kill 600 people. Two alternative programs to combat the disease have been proposed. Assume that the exact scientific estimates of the consequences of the program are as follows:
>
> If Program A is adopted, 200 people will be saved (chosen by 72%).
>
> If program B is adopted, there is a one-third probability that 600 people will be saved, and a two-thirds probability that no people will be saved (chosen by 28%).

Other subjects read the same description of the problem, followed by a different description of the consequences of the two programs.

> If Program A is adopted, 400 people will die (chosen by 22%).
>
> If Program B is adopted, there is a one-third probability that nobody will die and a two-thirds probability that 600 people will die (chosen by 78%).[2]

Thus, by restating the consequences of the alternative programs in terms of potential losses ("will die") rather than potential gains ("will be saved"), the structure of preferences was reversed even though the choices were identical.

Similarly, preferences for tax policies can be manipulated by framing the financial outcomes differently. When the tax consequences of family size were formulated as benefits (i.e., a tax credit would be allowed for children), few respondents favored a policy that would differentiate between rich and poor taxpayers in determining the amount of the credit available to either group. When the identical outcomes were phrased in terms of penalties (i.e., the tax rate would be lower, but there would be a surcharge for childlessness), respondents overwhelmingly favored imposing greater penalties on the rich.[3]

Framing effects have also been detected in nonlaboratory settings. For instance, physicians and patients were both considerably less attracted to surgery as a treatment for cancer when the statistics describing the results of the surgery were presented in terms of mortality rather than survival rates.[4] Similarly, Thaler has noted that the oil companies are apparently sensitive to the repellant aspects of phrasing choices in terms of penalties: the lower prices for gasoline offered to cash-paying customers are invariably expressed as a cash discount rather than as a credit card penalty.[5]

 Framing should be particularly significant as a determinant of choice when the choice problem involves politics. Political issues are typically complex, political discourse is ambiguous, and levels of public knowledge about and interest in politics are low.[6] In the area of public opinion, the impact of framing has been examined by survey researchers concerned with the stability of opinion responses across alternative question forms. These studies have shown that unobtrusive alterations in the wording and form of survey questions produce dramatic variations in opinions.[7] For example, Americans are generally tolerant of dissent when survey questions frame dissent as a general democratic right but are significantly less tolerant when the questions direct their attention to specific dissenting groups.[8] In the area of social welfare policy, the percentage of respondents favoring more generous governmental cash assistance is markedly higher if the recipients of the assistance are said to be "poor people" rather than "people on welfare."[9]

The framing effects detected in experimental and survey studies emerge across a wide range of subject matter sophistication and expertise.[10] Thus, it cannot be concluded that framing effects are limited to the naive and the ignorant. Nor can it be argued that framing effects are limited to judgments about trivial matters, for, as the nonlaboratory studies demonstrate, framing effects also apply to judgments of considerable personal relevance. As Kahneman and Tversky noted, "In their stubborn appeal, framing effects resemble perceptual illusions rather than computational errors."[11]

The impact of contextual cues other than question wording has received little attention from political scientists. If language variations are capable of influencing opinion responses so powerfully, however, it seems likely that alternate forms of television news presentations should also evoke similar variability in political choices and preferences. The remainder of this chapter describes the formats, or frames, in which network news is generally presented.

How Television News Frames Political Issues

The studies described here were based on the premise that all television news stories can be classified (based on the format of presentation) as either "episodic" or "thematic." The episodic news frame takes the form of a case study or event-oriented report and depicts public issues in terms of concrete instances (for example, the plight of a homeless person or a teenage drug user, the bombing of an airliner, or an attempted murder). The thematic frame, by contrast, places public issues in some more general or abstract context and takes the form of a "takeout," or "backgrounder," report directed at general outcomes or conditions. Examples of thematic coverage include reports on changes in government welfare expenditures, congressional debates over the funding of employment training programs, the social or political grievances of groups undertaking terrorist activity, and the backlog in the criminal justice process. The essential difference between episodic and thematic framing is that episodic framing depicts concrete events that illustrate issues, while thematic framing presents collective or general evidence. Visually, episodic reports make "good pictures," while thematic reports feature "talking heads."[12]

In practice, few news reports are exclusively episodic or thematic. Even the most detailed, close-up look at a particular poor person, for instance, invariably includes lead-in remarks by the anchorperson or reporter on the scope of poverty nationwide. Conversely, an account of the legislative struggle over budgetary cuts in social welfare programs might include a brief scene of children in a day-care center scheduled to close as the result of the funding cuts. For most stories, however, one frame or the other clearly predominates. (The issue of mixed frames is given further attention in chapter 3.)

Television news is essentially a twenty-one-minute "headline service" operating under powerful commercial dictates and well-defined norms of journalistic objectivity.[13] These constraints of time, advertising, and professional ethics explain why most television news reports focus on concrete acts and breaking events. Episodic reports present on-the-scene coverage of "hard" news and are often visually compelling. Thematic coverage of related background material would require in-depth, interpretive analysis, which would take longer to prepare and would be more susceptible to charges of journalistic bias. Moreover, there simply is not airtime available to present thematic background on all issues deemed newsworthy.

The dominance of the episodic frame in television news has been established in a number of studies. For example, television news coverage of mass-protest movements generally focuses more closely on specific acts of protest than on the issues that gave rise to the protests. This pattern characterized network coverage of the protests against the Vietnam War and of the development of nuclear energy.[14] The identical pattern is observed in television news coverage of labor-management disputes, where scenes of picketing workers received more airtime than discussions of the economic and political grievances at stake.[15] Event-oriented stories also account for most news coverage of international terrorism; information about specific terrorist acts is not accompanied by information about their underlying historical, economic, or social antecedents.[16] Altheide has observed that television news coverage of the Iran hostage crisis

> was reduced to one story—the freeing of the hostages—rather
> than coverage of its background and context, of the
> complexities of Iran, of alternative American policies, and of
> contemporary parochial politics in a world dominated by
> superpowers. Such messages were not forthcoming in the face
> of counts of the number of days of captivity and more footage of
> angry demonstrators and emotional relatives of hostages.[17]

Finally, the networks' preference for episodic reporting also emerges in the coverage of election campaigns. It is commonly accepted that the campaign, as described by television news, is primarily a "horse race." Stories on the latest standings in the polls, delegate counts, and the size of the crowd at a public rally appear far more frequently than coverage of the ideological stances of the candidates and the policy platforms they advocate.[18]

Existing scholarship on media framing has been primarily concerned with describing patterns of news coverage and identifying the economic, organizational, and other characteristics of the broadcasting business that produce the demand for episodic news. These studies have generally not attempted to address the specific effects of alternative news frames on the political choices of the viewing audience.[19]

The research to be reported here examines the impact of television news framing of six contemporary political issues—international terrorism, crime, poverty, unemployment, racial inequality, and the Reagan administration's "Iran-Contra" dealings—on attributions of political responsibility. The results indicate that the use of either the episodic or the thematic news frame affects how individuals assign responsibility for political issues; briefly, episodic framing tends to elicit individualistic rather than societal attributions of responsibility, while thematic framing has the opposite effect. Since television news is heavily episodic, its effect is generally to induce attributions of responsibility to individual victims or perpetrators rather than to broad societal forces, and hence the ultimate political impact of framing is proestablishment.

THREE

Methods of Research

The importance of using multiple methods in communications research has been long acknowledged but seldom practiced.[1] Multiple methods permit the researcher to reject with greater confidence the possibility that evidence is artifactual.

The present work adopts a multiple-method strategy and presents evidence drawn from content analysis, field experiments, and correlational analysis of national surveys. Content analysis is used to identify the degree of thematic or episodic framing in television news coverage of public issues. Field experiments provide a rigorous test of the impact of particular news frames on attributions of responsibility. National surveys provide generalizable evidence concerning the effect of attributions of responsibility on political opinions and attitudes.

The Sample of Issues

The direction in which people attribute responsibility was expected to differ across issue areas. For some issues, government or society might be held primarily responsible for both cause and treatment, while for other issues, either private actors or some combination of private and public entities might be held primarily responsible.

This research examined attributions of responsibility with respect to two major categories of issues and a specific governmental decision. The two categories were public security (or law-and-order) issues, and issues of social or economic welfare. The law-and-order category consisted of crime and terrorism. The social welfare category consisted of the specific issues of poverty, unemployment, and racial inequality. These five issues have been perennials in recent American politics. The research also examined news coverage of the most controversial governmental decision of recent years—the Reagan administration's sale of military equipment and supplies to Iran.

Content Analysis

Content analysis may be defined as a systematic effort to classify textual material. The "texts" described here are the *Abstracts* of the daily network newscasts compiled by the Television News Archive at Vanderbilt University. The "sample" consists of an abstract of every news story aired by ABC, CBS, and NBC between January 1981 and December 1986 bearing on each of the issues under investigation. The stories were retrieved using a key-word search; that is, for each issue, a list of relevant key words was prepared, and all stories referring to any of the words were selected for examination. In the case of poverty, for example, the key words included "welfare," "hunger," "malnutrition," "homeless," "elderly," "disabled," "Medicare," and "dependent children."

For all five of the perennial issues, every story retrieved was found to fit into either episodic or thematic framing categories. The episodic category (which proved most frequent) consisted of stories that depicted issues predominantly as concrete instances or events, while the thematic category included stories that depicted issues more generally either in terms of collective outcomes, public policy debates, or historical trends.

While the episodic and thematic framing categories were reasonably distinct and exhaustive, relatively few stories were purely episodic or thematic. A news story on rising unemployment figures nationwide, for instance, might also, in addition to considering the implications of unemployment for the national economy (thematic framing), take a close-up look at an unemployed auto worker on welfare (episodic framing). Conversely, even the most detailed, close-up look at a poor person would include lead-in remarks by the anchorperson concerning poverty as a general problem. News stories were thus classified based on the predominant frame, which was initially determined by reference to the word count in the text of the *Abstracts*. Thus, a story concerning poverty would be classified as thematic only if the thematic frame predominated. The *Abstracts* are highly condensed summaries of news story transcripts. In order to assess the accuracy of the classifications based on the number of words devoted to episodic or thematic framing, a more detailed and "visual" content analysis was carried out with respect to all CBS stories broadcast on poverty and a representative sample of CBS stories broadcast on unemployment and terrorism (CBS was selected because at the time its national newscast had the largest audience.) The actual airtime devoted to thematic and episodic coverage was recorded. The results of the classification based on this more-detailed analysis indicated that the great majority of news stories were in fact skewed predominantly in the direction of either the thematic or episodic format. Stories classified as episodic based on the *Abstracts*, for example, were found to devote, on average, nearly 80 percent of their total airtime to episodic coverage. The visual analyses thus served to validate the text-based classification of news stories. (For additional details of the content analyses, see appendix A; the visual analyses are also discussed in chapters 4 and 5.)

Field Experiments

The logic of experimental research is disarmingly simple. The researcher manipulates some variable and then observes the effects, if any, on the phenomenon under investigation.[2] The experiments described here were all designed to manipulate how political issues are framed in television newscasts. In Poverty Experiment 1, for instance, one group of experimental participants watched episodic framing of poverty, while another group watched thematic framing.

The random assignment of participants to the two experimental conditions virtually guarantees that any difference between the groups results from the experimental manipulation, i.e., the news frames; if participants who saw thematic coverage assigned responsibility to society, under conditions of random assignment this difference would be attributed to framing.[3]

Procedure

The participants in the nine media framing experiments were residents of the Three Village area of Suffolk County (Eastern Long Island, New York) who were recruited through newspaper and other advertisements that offered ten dollars in return for participation in "television research." When participants arrived at the Media Research Laboratory (located on the campus of the State University of New York at Stony Brook), they were told that the object of the research was to investigate "selective perception," and that they were to watch a randomly selected compilation of news stories that had been broadcast during the past year.[4] They would then be asked to complete a questionnaire regarding their reactions to and evaluations of the news reports. This explanation, though false in its description of the object of the research, was plausible because the questionnaire did include several questions probing "thoughts, reactions, and feelings" to particular news stories.

After receiving their instructions, participants completed an informed consent form and a short pretest questionnaire concerning their personal background, level of political involvement, media activities, and party preference. They then watched a twenty-minute videotape consisting of seven news stories that were described as a representative selection of network news stories that had been broadcast during the past six months. In fact, the stories were actual news reports that had been previously broadcast by one of the three major networks. The fourth story on the tape represented the experimental manipulation. This story framed one of the six target issues in accordance with the experimental design. The length of this "treatment" story ranged between two and three minutes. With the exception of the treatment story, the videotapes were identical. On average, two participants were present for each viewing session.

On completion of the videotape, the participants completed a lengthy posttest (individually, in separate rooms) that included questions probing their attributions of causal and treatment responsibility for the "target" issue as well as numerous other questions concerning their policy preferences; their perceptions of President Reagan's issue positions; their assessments of the president's overall performance, his performance concerning specific issues, his competence, and his integrity; and their evaluations of various public figures, groups, and institutions. On completing the posttest questionnaire, participants were debriefed in full and paid.[5]

Measures

For each issue, attributions of causal and treatment responsibility were elicited with open-ended survey questions. Specifically, individuals were asked, "In your opinion, what are the most important causes of _____?" They were then asked, "If you were asked to suggest ways to reduce _____, what would you suggest?" Each individual was allowed to answer freely, without prompting.[6] Up to four separate responses were coded for each question. Although these responses were unwieldy and coding-intensive, they had the advantage of nonreactivity; unlike fixed-choice survey items, open-ended questions do not cue respondents to think of particular causes or treatments. Two coders read each questionnaire and classified each response. Despite the large number of "raw" categories, inter-coder agreement was more than acceptable (see appendix A).

Sampling Bias

The Achilles' heel of experimental research is, of course, the representativeness of experimental samples. In this case, the people who chose to participate in the studies constituted a reasonable approximation of the local area, i.e., Suffolk County, New York (see table 3.1). Unlike the typical social psychological experiment, university undergraduates were systematically excluded from the pool of participants.[7] Nonetheless, Suffolk County is hardly a microcosm of the nation. Compared with a representative sample of the American electorate, participants in the framing experiments tended to be more educated, more Catholic and Jewish, more affluent, and somewhat more likely to have voted in the last presidential election. Given these differences, it is especially important that the experimental results be replicated with broader, more representative national samples. The research therefore includes parallel survey analyses of several experimental findings.

Realism versus Precision

One of the costs of realistic experimental manipulations is a certain loss in precision. The critical framing manipulation described earlier compared viewers' responses to *different* news stories. Every effort was made to make the treatment stories equivalent in information and presentation. They were edited (using state-of-the-art facilities) so as to be identical in length. The anchors' lead-in remarks were similarly edited to achieve maximum content similarity. When the treatment stories were taken from the same network, the identical lead-in was used. Similar precautions were undertaken to minimize

Table 3.1 Participant Profile

	Experimental Participants (%)	1980 NES National Sample (%)	1980 Suffolk County[a] (%)
Female	56	57	51
Nonwhite	7	13	8
High school graduates	37	63	64
College	33	20	18
College graduates	30	17	18
Employed	71	56	58
Unemployed	7	8	6
Retired	5	13	
Housewife	7	18	} 36
Student	8	3	
Blue collar	24	37	27
White collar	54	31	48
Professional	22	22	26
Protestant	36	63	*
Roman Catholic	42	23	*
Jewish	16	3	*
Voted in last election	68	62	*
Republican	25	22	37
Democratic	32	41	23
Independent	29	24	23
N	772	965	

Note: The median age for the experimental participants, the NES respondents, and Suffolk County residents was 34, 41, and 31 respectively.

   [a]Suffolk County data provided by Long Island Regional Planning Board.

   *Data not available.

differences between the treatment stories in their potential for viewer attentiveness or engagement.

Nonetheless, the framing manipulation consisted of nonidentical stimuli. To guard against the possibility that the experimental results were produced by mere idiosyncratic or content differences in treatment stories rather than by differences in framing, the experimental conditions were compared in terms of two indicators of viewer involvement—the total number of responses to the open-ended cause and treatment questions and the level of emotion aroused by the stories. In not one study did a robust difference occur across experimental conditions in the total number of causal and treatment responses, and in only two instances did experimental conditions differ noticeably in the number of emotions elicited.[8] The treatment stories thus did not generally differ in their ability to trigger open-ended comments or arouse emotions. Finally, to further guard against the possibility of spurious results, the experimental tests of framing were generally replicated using an entirely different set of stories.

In short, the framing manipulation used here is not as rigorous as that used in the psychological laboratory. The use of actual (as opposed to contrived) news stories created extraneous differences between the different news frames; however, by constraining the treatment news stories to a high degree of audio-visual homogeneity and by pursuing a strategy of replication, the role of these differences was minimized. To the degree the observed framing effects emerge across different manipulations, the possibility that idiosyncratic differences between the news stories are at work is minimized.

Avoiding Experimental Demand

In any experimental procedure it is imperative that the researcher minimize the effects of demand characteristics—i.e., cues in the experimental situation or procedure that suggest to participants what is expected of them.[9] Several such precautions were undertaken here, including the previously mentioned description of the study which, though credible, effectively disguised its true intent.

In addition, treatment stories were compiled using studio-quality editing equipment (with three-quarter-inch videotapes) so that participants could not detect the alterations to the news reports. Moreover, the manipulations were realistic in that the stories used were actual stories that had previously been broadcast by ABC, CBS, or NBC. The use of open-ended questions to probe attributions of responsibility made it relatively difficult for participants to infer what the researcher was looking for.

The aura of the research laboratory was reduced (and the economic incentives to participate were raised) by encouraging prospective participants to come in pairs with a spouse, friend, or colleague. The average session size of two meant that, typically, participants watched the videotape in the presence of a companion. In addition, participants could sip coffee or browse through newspapers and magazines. Finally, concern over experimental demand also dictated the choice of a posttest-only design. (Had the questions about attributions of responsibility been included in the pretest and posttest, participants would have been alerted to the objective of the experiment.)

Correlational Analysis

The effects of framing on attributions of political responsibility are of interest chiefly because such attributions, in turn, powerfully influence public opinion. In this research, correlational analysis was used to explore the connection between attributions and opinions. These investigations were carried out using the data obtained from the Suffolk County experiments and various national surveys administered by the Center for Political Studies (of the University of Michigan) and polls administered by the *New York Times* and "CBS News."

The opinions examined in the survey analyses fell into two categories. *General evaluations of government* included questions concerning the president's overall performance in office, his competence, and his integrity. *Issue-specific opinions* included evaluations of the president's performance in specific issue areas (e.g., reducing unemployment), respondents' specific policy preferences (e.g., support for additional federal spending on civil rights programs), and, finally, respondents' affect for a variety of groups and individuals (e.g., poor people, the police, Colonel Qaddafi) within each of the target issue areas.

This section of the analysis also examined the effects of several personal characteristics on political opinions (see appendix C). Political party identification and liberal-conservative orientation are generally thought to be the most relevant of such "long-term" or dispositional opinion cues; in all of the survey analyses described below, partisan and ideological differences were taken into account in both general political evaluations and issue-specific opinions.

In addition to partisanship and ideological orientation, factual knowledge may also serve to guide political opinions. People differ considerably in their level of information about political issues. Although there is no specific theoretical basis or body of evidence to suggest that those who are politically informed and those who are not express different opinions, the analysis nonetheless incorporated a measure of factual information about the target issues in order to eliminate the possibility that the effects of attribution of responsibility on public opinion were merely the effects of information in disguise. Finally, the survey analysis also controlled for the effects of socioeconomic status on political opinions.

The survey analyses proceeded in two stages. First, the impact of attributions on opinions and attitudes within specific issue areas were assessed (chapter 7). For instance, this analysis revealed significant differences in social welfare policy preferences between individuals attributing responsibility for poverty to society and those attributing responsibility to the poor. In effect, this stage of the analysis indicates how well attributions of responsibility perform as *domain-specific* opinion cues. Second, the impact of attributions on general evaluations of the president were assessed (chapter 8). In effect, this stage of the analysis indicates how well attributions of responsibility perform as *general* opinion cues.

FOUR

Effects of Framing on Attributions of Responsibility for Crime and Terrorism

On the surface, crime and terrorism appear to be similar political issues because both entail threats to public security. Crime, however, is the more immediate danger and, for many, is a matter of intense personal experience, providing a dramatic connection between everyday life and the affairs of society at large. The threat posed by terrorism is generally distant and remote. Indeed, terrorism is the prototypical mediated issue, public awareness is limited to scenes of aircraft hijackings, hostage situations, bombings, and similar dramas played out in the mass media. Though spectacular, these events are of little direct personal relevance.

Differences in the relative obtrusiveness of the two issues has important implications for the framing hypothesis. Because crime is a real personal threat, citizens were expected to have more intimate familiarity with the issue, and attributions of responsibility for crime were expected to be less responsive to contextual cues such as framing. In contrast, because terrorism is associated with poorly understood disputes in distant locales and with ideological conflicts, attributions of responsibility for terrorism were expected to be highly responsive to framing. In short, media influence on attribution was expected to be more powerful for terrorism than for crime.

How Television News Frames Crime and Terrorism

Crime and terrorism, especially the latter, were at the forefront of the networks' issue agenda in the 1980s. Some eleven hundred news reports on crime and more than two thousand reports on terrorism were aired by ABC, CBS, and NBC between 1981 and 1986. The average of eleven stories on terrorism per month for each network represented an unusually intense degree of coverage. Between 1981 and 1986, more stories were broadcast on terrorism than on poverty, unemployment, racial inequality, and crime combined. Hijackings, hostage situations, and similar events have been emblazoned on the public consciousness.

The networks framed crime and terrorism almost exclusively in episodic terms (see figure 4.1). Eight-nine percent of all news stories on crime fell into this "police-blotter" format.[1] Within both the thematic and episodic categories, the news tended to focus on violent crime. Thus, the focus of the typical news report was a specific individual (perpetrator or victim) and a violent criminal act.

Although news coverage of terrorism was slightly more thematic than coverage for crime, episodic reports still outnumbered thematic reports by a ratio of three to one: 74 percent of all news stories on terrorism consisted of live reports of some specific terrorist act, group, victim, or event, while 26 percent consisted of reports that discussed terrorism as a general political problem (see appendix A). These results are consistent with prior content analyses performed by others, which identified a strong "event" bias in network treatment of terrorism.[2] These researchers have speculated that the event bias and the concomitant inattention to general, background information occurs because of the dramatic qualities of news stories on terrorist acts. As Altheide argues:

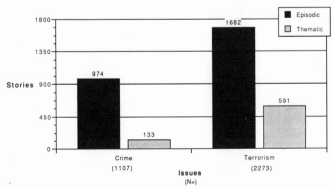

Fig. 4.1 Episodic and Thematic Coverage of Crime and Terrorism, 1981–86

Television reports that rely on visuals of an event will be more entertaining to an audience, yet provide little useful narrative interpretation to understand the broader issue. As long as more dramatic visuals are associated with the tactics and aftermath of terrorism, these aspects will be stressed over the larger issues of history, goals, and rationale.[3]

Episodic and thematic treatments of terrorism were examined within specific subject matter categories. Episodic reports were classified by the nationality of the subject individual(s), group(s), or organization(s). Third-world nationals accounted for 51 percent of episodic stories; within this group, Middle Easterners received the most attention, followed by Central Americans. Western terrorists were also the subject of extensive coverage, accounting for 34 percent of episodic stories.

Thirty-three percent of the thematic news reports focused on the U.S. government's counter-terrorist efforts. The remaining thematic stories were widely scattered in subject matter focus.

Who Is Responsible?

Crime elicited the highest average number of causal and treatment attributions of responsibility (2.7 and 2.1 per respondent, respectively) of any of the issues examined (see figure 4.2). Presumably, people had more to say about crime because crime is more of a "doorstep" issue than terrorism, poverty, unemployment, or racial inequality.

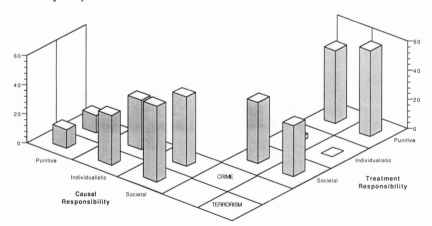

Fig. 4.2 Causal and Treatment Attribution of Responsibility for Crime and Terrorism

Causal responsibility for both crime and terrorism was assigned to the individuals who commit criminal or terrorist acts, to a variety of societal conditions, and to a lack of adequate punitive policies.[4] Individualistic attributions for crime consisted of two causal themes—character deficiencies (such as greed, personality disorders, and the desire to avoid working) and inadequate education and employment skills. Individualistic attributions for terrorism consisted exclusively of character references, primarily political fanaticism and associated personality traits, such as lack of concern for human life and a craving for power. The level of individualistic attributions of causal responsibility was virtually identical for crime and terrorism (38 and 34 percent, respectively).

References to society in causal attributions for crime and terrorism consisted of two opposing themes. Participants either referred to a variety of social, economic, or political conditions that fostered crime and terrorism or to society's failure to punish adequately those who engage in criminal or terrorist acts. The former category was labelled societal causal responsibility, and the latter punitive causal responsibility.

Attributions of societal causal responsibility for crime included references to economic conditions, discrimination, racial inequality, poverty, and cultural institutions. The category of cultural institutions was reserved for responses that cited the role of the mass media and the entertainment industry in glamorizing crime and legitimizing the use of violence. Societal causes of terrorism included economic and political oppression, the actions and policies of the U.S. government (including support for Israel, insufficient economic aid to underprivileged nations, siding with repressive leaders, and realpolitik), global politics (such as meddling by the superpowers and other nations, most notably, Libya), and local political turmoil (including breakdown of institutions, political strife, and lack of strong leadership). Societal attributions represented 48 and 52 percent of all attributions of causal responsibility for crime and terrorism, respectively.

Punitive causal responsibility—the argument that people engage in crime and terrorism because they are able to avoid severe punishment—was infrequently mentioned. Approximately 10 percent of all causal responses for both issues referred to the lack of adequate punitive measures.

Respondents assigned treatment responsibility for both crime and terrorism almost exclusively to society in general. Very few responses implied that self-improvement was an appropriate treatment, indicating that apparently individuals do not view criminals and terrorists as able or willing to mend their ways. Thus, the prescription for crime and terrorism was almost exclusively improvements in the underlying socioeconomic and political order (societal treatment responsibility), or the imposition of stricter and more certain punishment (punitive treatment responsibility).

Societal treatments suggested for crime included reductions in poverty and inequality, rehabilitative and educational programs, and an improved economy. Respondents also cited heightened public awareness ("form neighborhood crime-prevention groups"; "educate people on ways to avoid being a victim") as a potential treatment. These four categories made up 42 percent of all crime treatments mentioned. In the case of terrorism, suggested societal treatments included resolution of terrorists' political grievances, putting an end to oppression, the use of more responsive methods of negotiating with terrorists, and greater public awareness (for example, "provide tourists with information regarding political conditions"). Societal responsibility accounted for 35 percent of the treatment responses directed at terrorism.

The dominant prescription for both issues (both in terms of content and frequency) called for the imposition of more severe retaliation or punishment against terrorists and criminals (punitive treatment responsibility). This category accounted for nearly 66 percent of all treatment responses for terrorism and 50 percent of all treatment responses directed at crime.

The degree to which causal and treatment responses corresponded within each issue was also examined by constructing dichotomized "net" causal and treatment responsibility scores. In the case of causal responsibility, low scores indicate a tendency to cite individual characteristics or inadequate punishment as causes; high scores indicate a tendency to assign causal responsibility to prevailing societal conditions. In the case of treatment responsibility, low scores represent a preference for attributions of punitive responsibility, while high scores represent a preference for attributions of societal responsibility (see appendix B).

By combining the causal and treatment responsibility scores, a four-fold typology was identified, as follows:

1. Deterrence model: individual tendencies and insufficient pun-

ishment cause crime and terrorism; stronger punishment of criminals and terrorists is the treatment.

2. Societal model: inadequate societal conditions cause crime and terrorism; improvements in societal conditions are the treatment.
3. Guardianship model: individual tendencies and insufficient punishment are the primary causal factors; improvements in societal conditions are the treatment.
4. Punitive model: inadequate societal conditions cause crime and terrorism; stronger punishment is the appropriate treatment.

Figure 4.3 shows the number and percentage of participants falling within each of the above models. For both issues, the deterrence model was applied most frequently and, in the case of crime, attracted close to 50 percent of the sample. The societal and guardianship models were applied to terrorism more frequently (by small margins) than to crime. The punitive model of responsibility attracted less than 20 percent of the sample for both issues. Overall, the pattern of causal and treatment responsibility for crime and terrorism was similar.[5]

Experimental Tests of Framing

Terrorism Experiment 1

This study was essentially an exploratory probe of individuals' causal attributions. The experimental manipulation focused on a specific terrorist event—the hijacking of TWA Flight 847 and the ensuing hostage situation in Beirut.[6] Following the release of the hostages, all three networks broadcast detailed recapitulations of the

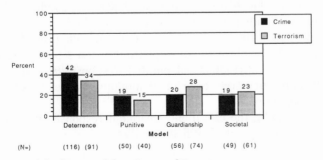

Fig. 4.3 Models of Responsibility: Crime and Terrorism

crisis. The ABC report was edited into three very different versions. Two of the reports embodied a thematic frame, while the third represented the more frequently encountered episodic frame.

The first thematic framing condition, "U.S. Foreign Policy," interpreted the hijacking incident as an act of political protest against U.S. foreign policy. The report commented on the role of the United States as a traditional ally of Israel and the hijackers' demands that Israel release Lebanese citizens held as political prisoners. President Reagan was then shown declaring that the United States would never negotiate with terrorists.

The second thematic-framing condition, "Local Turmoil," examined the incident exclusively within the context of Lebanese political strife. The report discussed the breakdown of governmental authority and the rise of various Lebanese paramilitary organizations, including Amal, the Shiite organization holding the hostages. The group's ideology was described, and its growing influence noted. This condition made no reference to the United States, to Israel, or to the broader Middle East conflict.

The third condition was designed as a noninterpretive, episodic frame—"Hostages Released." The report merely announced the release of the hostages. Individual hostages were seen greeting each other prior to departing from Beirut. Some of the former hostages commented on their health and their treatment in captivity. This condition provided no particular perspective on the hijacking incident beyond describing the eventual outcome.

Finally, a fourth, "control" condition was added to the design. Individuals assigned to this condition saw no news of the TWA hijacking. In place of the hijacking, they watched a story describing recent developments in the U.S. space program.

The major objective of this study was to examine the possibility that alternative news frames for the identical act of terrorism might induce shifts in attributions of responsibility. First, it was expected that thematic framing would induce viewers to attribute responsibility for terrorism to societal factors while episodic framing was expected to contribute to higher levels of individual or punitive responsibility. In addition, it was anticipated that viewers in the control condition would seize upon individual responsibility in their explanations of terrorism—the terrorist's fanaticism, evil intent, amorality, and other related traits. This prediction was derived from attribution theory, which suggests that people typically exaggerate the role of individuals' motives and intentions and simultaneously discount the role of contextual factors when attributing responsibility for individuals' actions, a tendency that psychologists have dubbed "the fundamental attribution error."[7]

In order to examine framing effects on attributions of causal responsibility for terrorism, indices of societal, punitive, and individualistic responsibility were computed corresponding to the number of responses that referred to these themes divided by the total number of responses (fig. 4.4). In the case of societal causal responsibility, for example, the index was the percentage of causal attributions citing political oppression or other societal factors (see appendix B). The use of such a standardized indicator of attribution served to neutralize possible differences in respondents' writing ability, locquacity, political interest, and related skills.

The degree to which attributions of causal responsibility for terrorism were affected by the particular news frame is shown in figure 4.4. As expected, societal attributions were least prominent when the hijacking was framed in episodic terms, and the episodic condition differed significantly from the thematic Local Turmoil condition (see

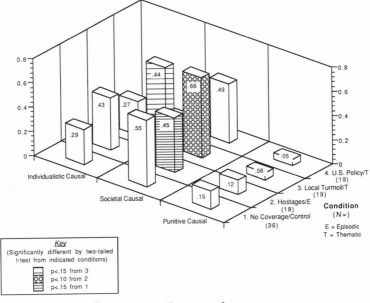

Fig. 4.4 Framing Effects: Terrorism Experiment 1

appendix B). Contrary to expectations, however, the two thematic conditions did not elicit an equivalent pattern of responses. The frequency of individualistic attributions was highest in the thematic U.S. Foreign Policy condition and lowest in the thematic Local Turmoil condition. As a result, the two thematic conditions differed significantly in the level of individualistic attributions.[8]

Another surprising result was that individuals in the control condition attributed causal responsibility to society rather than to the individual terrorist. Rather than making the "fundamental attribution error," individuals who were given no information about terrorism tended to think of the issue as a product of social or political problems.

Finally, there were no differences between the four conditions in the proportion of viewers citing punitive responsibility. The level of punitive treatment responsibility did not exceed 15 percent in any of the experimental conditions.

Thus the results from the initial study are at least suggestive of network framing. Thematic framing of terrorism that placed an airplane hijacking in the context of local political upheaval raised the prominence of societal causal attributions. When the same hijacking was framed in episodic terms, characteristics of individual terrorists were at the forefront of viewers' attributions.

Terrorism Experiment 2

The second terrorism study was designed as a broader replication of the initial results. Seven conditions were established, three of which represented thematic framing and four episodic. All three thematic framing conditions were directed, in varying degrees and contexts, at U.S. governmental policies. Three of the four episodic framing conditions focused on terrorist acts in the Third World, while the fourth described a terrorist bombing in Great Britain.

The first thematic framing condition, "U.S. Counter-Terrorism Policy," described President Reagan's recently announced "war on terrorism." The report covered several policy options under consideration, ranging from economic sanctions against governments aiding terrorists to military reprisals. The reporter noted that a "tough" stance on terrorism had bipartisan congressional support. President Reagan was shown on screen declaring that he was "determined to fight this new barbarism."

The two other thematic framing conditions dealt with two particular regional hotbeds of terrorist activity. In the "Middle East–Thematic" condition, the anchor began by reporting an Israeli bombing raid against Lebanese villages said (by the Israelis) to be terrorist havens. The report then discussed the increasing internal strife in Lebanon following the Israeli invasion of that country. An Israeli government spokesman was asked questions concerning the policy of military retaliation and emphatically declared that Israel's actions were consistent with U.S. objectives in the region.

In the third thematic condition, "Central America–Thematic," the anchor began with the disclosure that the U.S.-backed Contra forces had distributed a "terrorism manual" to their units that had been allegedly prepared with Central Intelligence Agency collaboration. The report then surveyed the state of the Nicaraguan civil war, noting the high level of noncombatant casualties inflicted by both sides. A Contra spokesman denied charges that the Contras had made attacks against civilians. A prominent congressman reacted to the charges by noting that U.S. support for terrorist activity in Central America would be a foreign policy "disaster."

Three of the four episodic conditions focused on Third World participants. In the first such condition, "Arab Hijacker," the report described the hijacking of an Egypt Air plane and the subsequent assault on the aircraft by Egyptian commandoes, resulting in the deaths of sixty passengers, including several Americans. Two survivors described their ordeal. The reporter stated that the alleged hijacker was "Arab" and that a Libyan-backed splinter group of the Palestine Liberation Organization had claimed responsibility for the hijacking.

The second episodic-coverage condition, "Sikh Saboteurs," described the crash of a Air India Boeing 747 under mysterious circumstances, prompting widespread suspicion that a bomb had been placed on board by Sikh extremists. The two principal suspects, both active in the Sikh separatist movement, were described. The report ended with film of militant Sikhs demonstrating in New Delhi against the Indian government.

The third episodic condition, "Central American Insurgents," described the killing of six Americans, including three off-duty marines by "The Front for National Liberation" in San Salvador. Witnesses described the attack, the bodies of the victims were shown on screen, and the reporter noted the increasing frequency of such terrorist attacks in El Salvador.

Finally, the fourth episodic condition, "IRA Bombers," consisted of a report on an Irish Republican Army plot to kill Prime Minister Thatcher and several members of her cabinet. A Scotland Yard official announced the discovery of several sophisticated explosive devices at the site of the annual Conservative Party conference and described efforts to trace the IRA members involved. A cabinet member commented on the increasing dangers of holding public office in Great Britain.

In summary, the design of the second terrorism study was faithful to the major undercurrents of network news coverage—U.S. policy toward terrorism in the case of thematic framing and the Middle East, Central America, and Western Europe, as the principal arenas of terrorist activity in the case of episodic framing. The results of this study are shown in figure 4.5.

The three thematic conditions yielded similar and generally low levels of individualistic causal attributions but differed among themselves in the level of societal attributions. The Middle East–Thematic condition elicited the highest level of societal causal at-

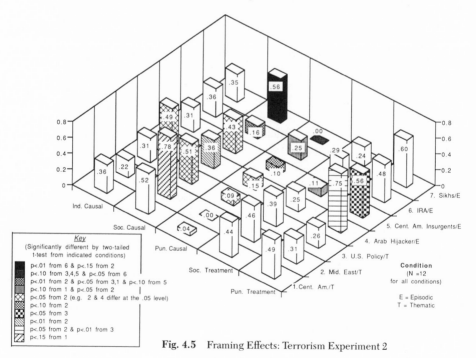

Fig. 4.5 Framing Effects: Terrorism Experiment 2

tributions (78 percent) and differed significantly from both other thematic conditions. The Middle East–Thematic condition also elicited significantly fewer references to punitive causal responsibility than the U.S. Counter-Terrorism Policy thematic condition. The three thematic conditions elicited a uniform pattern of responses for attributions of treatment responsibility. Thematic framing tended to polarize treatment responses; in all three thematic conditions, the ratio of punitive to societal treatment responses was roughly equal.

The episodic conditions proved diverse in their effects on causal attributions but were homogeneous in their effects on treatment attributions. The IRA Bombers condition elicited a distinctively high proportion (25 percent) of punitive causal attributions and a correspondingly low proportion of societal causal attributions. The Sikh Saboteurs condition had precisely the opposite effect, drawing extensive attributions of societal causal responsibility and, despite the large number of people killed, no reference whatsoever to inadequate punitive measures. In this latter respect, the Sikh Saboteurs condition differed significantly from the three remaining episodic conditions.

Because the episodic conditions differed among themselves in several respects (including the nationality of the terrorist group or individual(s), depicted, the terrorist tactic used, and the number of people killed), it is difficult to trace differences in responses within the episodic framing conditions to particular characteristics of the news reports. The distinctiveness of the IRA condition, however, may stem from the fact that contextual antecedents of terrorism—such as governmental instability and economic and social deprivation—do not apply so readily to a stable Western society like Great Britain. In other words, societal attributions may be prominent elements of individuals' "knowledge" about the causes of terrorism so long as the terrorists are from non-Western or less-developed countries. Confronted with instances of European terrorism, people turn to alternative causes such as the lack of adequate punitive measures.

Notwithstanding the preceding idiosyncratic differences within the episodic conditions, the overall pattern of differences between the episodic and thematic conditions provided strong evidence in support of framing. All four episodic conditions elicited lower levels of societal causal attributions than at least one of the thematic conditions, and all four episodic conditions pulled higher levels of punitive causal attributions than at least one of the thematic conditions. In the case of treatment responsibility, the Arab Hijacker condition induced a significantly higher level of punitive responsibility than two of the three thematic framing conditions. In addition, the Central American Insurgents condition elicited significantly fewer societal attributions than two of the thematic conditions and significantly more punitive attributions than the U.S. Counter-Terrorism Policy thematic condition. All told, differences between the episodic and thematic framing conditions far outnumbered differences within either category. There were seventeen statistically significant "inter-frame" differences, compared with only eight significant "intra-frame" differences. Figure 4.6 shows the effects of framing in this study by comparing the aggregated data from the thematic conditions with the aggregated data from the episodic conditions.

Collectively, the episodic and thematic framing conditions made for sharply diverging patterns of causal and treatment attributions. Causal attributions were primarily individualistic and punitive when the networks framed terrorism as a specific terrorist act; they were primarily societal when the networks framed terrorism as a general problem. Attributions of treatment responsibility were also strongly influenced by framing. Episodic framing elicited a much more one-sided distribution (in the direction of punitive responsibility) of responses than did thematic framing; the ratio of punitive to societal

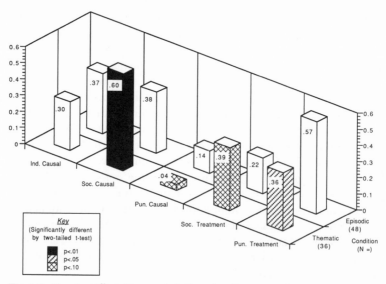

Fig. 4.6 Framing Effects (Aggregated): Terrorism Experiment 2

treatment attributions was nearly three to one under episodic framing but only one to one following thematic framing.

Finally, it is revealing to compare differences in the particular combinations of causal and treatment responsibility expressed following thematic and episodic framing of terrorism. Under conditions of episodic framing, 64 percent of viewers were found to fit the deterrence model of responsibility (individual causes coupled with punitive treatments) compared with only 33 percent of viewers in the thematic conditions. The discrepancy was even greater in the case of the societal model (societal causal and treatment responsibility). While this model attracted 25 percent of the participants in the thematic conditions, it accounted for only 5 percent of the sample in the episodic conditions.

Taken together, the two experiments on terrorism indicate that attributions of responsibility differ substantially depending upon episodic or thematic framing of the issue. When terrorism is depicted as a general outcome, viewers gravitate toward societal attributions. On the other hand, when terrorism is framed as a specific act or event, viewers gravitate toward individualistic and punitive attributions.

Crime Experiment 1

This experiment was designed to reflect the sheer dominance of violent crime in network news. Violent crime was depicted using either thematic or episodic framing. Thematic framing consisted of information about crime and victimization rates for the country or particular areas, elements of the criminal justice process, governmental or community responses to crime, and so forth. Episodic framing depicted a specific instance of violent crime. The thematic and episodic framing conditions were then further divided according to race, focusing alternatively on black or white crime. The distinction between black and white crime was based on the individuals or groups depicted as the perpetrators of criminal activity.

In the "Black Crime-Thematic" condition a feature report on "Crime in Black America" described the increasing rate of violent crime and the increasing number of crime victims in predominantly black inner-city areas of Chicago, Houston, Los Angeles, and New York. The reporter traced the economic decline of these areas since the 1960s, and a black civic leader commented that people living in the inner city faced conditions of "desperation."

In the "Black Crime–Episodic" condition, the news story described a violent confrontation between two black youth gangs in Los Angeles that resulted in seven deaths. Individual gang members were shown in police custody. The police chief of Los Angeles denounced the gangs, and the mother of one of the victims expressed her grief.

News coverage of white violent crime was also presented in thematic and episodic terms. In the "White Crime–Thematic" condition, the news report detailed the growing economic power of organized crime and identified some of the major groups involved in the struggle for control of the underworld. The assassinations of several prominent organized crime figures were cited as evidence of growing factional conflict. An FBI official speculated about the origins of the conflict and noted that governmental electronic surveillance of organized crime groups had been intensified.

In the "White Crime–Episodic" condition, the focus of the news report was directed at a well-known shooting in the New York City subway by a passenger, Bernhard Goetz. The reporter briefly summarized the incident, a clip of Bernhard Goetz's videotaped confession was shown, and Goetz stated in an interview that he would repeat his actions if placed in a similar situation. (Goetz shot a group of four unarmed black youths—injuring two of them seriously—who approached him in a "menacing" manner on the subway.)

Although violent crime was the major component of the study design, two additional categories of news stories on crime were incorporated—"Illegal Drugs" and "Criminal Justice Process." Stories about drugs were included simply because no other aspect of crime has commanded as much public (and media) attention in recent years. Coverage of the criminal justice process was included because prior research indicated that beliefs about the effectiveness of the criminal justice system influence individuals' attributions of responsibility.[9]

News coverage of illegal drugs and the criminal justice process were also framed in both thematic and episodic terms. The "Illegal Drugs–Thematic" condition consisted of a news report that described the significant increase in the consumption of heroin and cocaine-based substances nationwide. The reporter cited figures indicating the lucrativeness of the drug trade and interviewed a Justice Department official who noted that a significant portion of the drug trade was controlled by international crime organizations and that the Reagan administration's "War on Drugs" featured cooperative multi-government efforts to fight the problem.

The "Illegal Drugs–Episodic" condition consisted of a report on "Crack" that began with the anchor's lead-in statement concerning the growing number of Americans using this drug. The story then proceeded to describe two addicts—a black male New Yorker and a white female Midwesterner—and their unsuccessful efforts to break their drug dependence.

The "Criminal Justice Process–Thematic" condition was adapted from a "Special Segment" news report on "Crime in America" in which the U.S. crime rate was contrasted with that of other industrialized nations. The report highlighted the congestion in the courts, the high proportion of plea bargains, and the low percentage of criminals who are jailed. The reporter concluded that, given adequate legal counsel, crime "pays" in America.

The "Criminal Justice Process–Episodic" condition consisted of a report that described the outcome of two criminal cases in which well-known and wealthy defendants (former Louisiana Governor Edwin Edwards and boxing promoter Don King) were acquitted of felony charges. The report summarized the charges brought against Edwards (a white) and King (a black). The reporter interviewed a Justice Department official (concerning the outcome of the trials) who denied charges of leniency and lax prosecution.

In sum, the experimental manipulation consisted of four subject matter manipulations corresponding to news coverage of white violent crime, black violent crime, illegal drugs, and the criminal justice process. In all four manipulations, crime was framed either with thematic or episodic news reports. This design enabled investigation of several hypotheses going beyond the basic framing notion. The racial comparison, for instance, was designed to address the question of whether viewers would assign responsibility for crime differently depending on the race of the individual(s) seen engaging in criminal activity. The general expectation was that, while news coverage of black crime would tend to elicit a relatively lower level of societal responsibility, coverage of white crime would direct the predominantly white audience to attribute responsibility to society. This was a particularly strong expectation in the episodic framing comparison since Bernhard Goetz's actions were widely heralded in the local media as courageous and taken in self-defense.[10]

In addition to racial cuing in coverage of violent crime, news coverage of illegal drugs and the criminal justice process were expected to differ in their effects on attributions of responsibility. It is difficult to think about the problem of illegal drugs without considering individuals who use drugs, and coverage of drugs was therefore expected to highlight individual causal responsibility. News about the criminal justice process was expected to draw attention to procedural factors that enable law breakers to evade prosecution; therefore, it was expected that these reports would increase references to punitive causal and treatment responsibility.

Indices of individual, societal, and punitive causal responsibility were constructed in order to assess the impact of the subject matter and framing manipulations. Treatment responsibility was analyzed in terms of societal and punitive attributions (see appendix B). The observed differences among the four subject matter manipulations on the various measures of responsibility are shown in figure 4.7.

Societal attributions of causal responsibility were cited most frequently when the news focused on white violent crime. Societal attributions also appeared frequently when news coverage was directed at the criminal justice process. In contrast, societal attributions were mentioned least frequently when the news focused on black violent crime. The mean societal responsibility score of 29 percent in this condition differed significantly from all other subject matter conditions. News coverage of black crime not only diverted

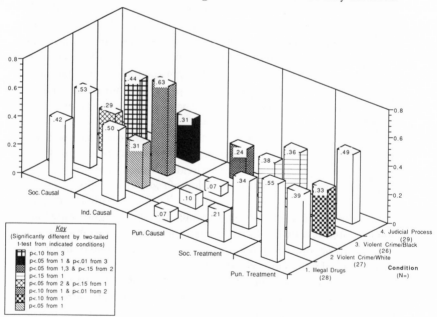

Fig. 4.7 Subject Matter Effects: Crime Experiment 1

attention from societal responsibility, but also attracted attention to individual responsibility. More than 60 percent of all causal attributions were directed at individuals when the news reported on black violent crime. This was *double* the comparable percentage in the White Crime condition. Once again, the Black Crime condition differed significantly from all other subject matter conditions.

News coverage of illegal drugs and the judicial process also affected causal attributions for crime. As expected, individualistic attributions of responsibility were more prominent following news coverage of illegal drugs. This condition differed significantly from both the Criminal Justice Process and White Crime conditions, where references to individual responsibility made up less than 33 percent of all causal attributions. The proportion of causal attributions citing inadequate punishment in the Criminal Justice Process condition was more than double the proportion in the remaining conditions.

The effects of variations in the subject matter of the news on attributions of treatment responsibility for crime were most visible in the Illegal Drugs condition. While societal responsibility accounted for only 20 percent of all treatment attributions in the Illegal Drugs condition, it accounted for nearly 40 percent of all treatment attributions when the news report concerned black crime or the judicial process. In addition, the Illegal Drugs condition induced the highest level of punitive treatment attributions and differed significantly from the Black Crime condition ($p < .10$).

Turning to the combined effects of subject matter and framing, the five indicators of responsibility were subjected to a four-by-two analysis of variance (four subject matter categories and two frames). (See figure 4.8.)

The effects of framing were erratic and generally overshadowed by the effects of subject matter coverage. Although episodic reports tended to elicit higher levels of individual causal attributions and punitive treatment attributions, neither of these "main effects" could be considered statistically significant; however, individual and punitive causal attributions, in addition to societal treatment attributions, were interactively affected by framing. Interaction effects refer to the joint, or combined, influence of subject matter and framing on attributions. In the case of individual causal responsibility, the interaction effect was significant; for punitive causal responsibility and societal treatment responsibility, the interaction effect approached statistical significance.

Thus, the effects of framing on individualistic causal attributions

Chapter Four

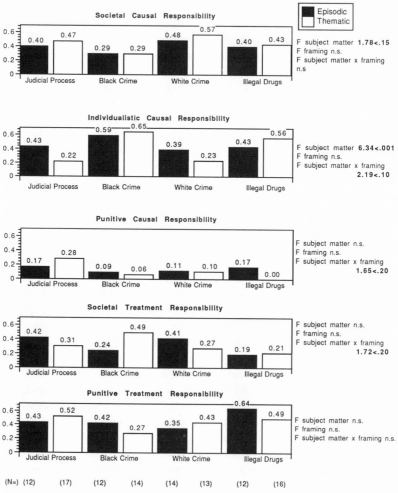

Fig. 4.8 Subject Matter and Framing Effects: Crime Experiment 1

depended upon the particular subject matter focus of the news. Episodic framing of white crime and the judicial process elicited significantly higher levels of individual responsibility than thematic framing, but framing effects were absent in the areas of black crime and illegal drugs. This inconsistency can be traced to the already dominant status of individual responsibility in the Black Crime and Illegal Drugs conditions. Where references to individual responsibility were not so prominent to begin with (as in the case of participants exposed to news about white crime and the criminal justice process) framing effects proved significant.

The marginally significant interaction effect in the case of societal treatment responsibility was traced to the Black Crime condition, where the thematic report (rising crime in black urban areas) elicited more than double the percentage of societal treatment attributions than the episodic report (gang warfare in Los Angeles). For the three remaining subject matter areas, there were no noticeable differences between episodic and thematic conditions.

Conclusion

As anticipated, framing was more powerful when terrorism was the target issue; the episodic versus thematic manipulations yielded strong results for terrorism, but only weak results for crime. The dominant episodic frame in network coverage encouraged viewers to attribute causal responsibility for terrorism to the personal qualities of terrorists and to the inadequacy of sanctions. Episodic framing also made viewers more likely to consider punitive measures rather than social or political reform as the appropriate treatment for terrorism. In the case of crime, the dominant episodic frame did increase attributions of individualistic causal responsibility and of punitive treatment responsibility, but these effects were contingent upon the subject matter focus of the news. Episodic framing made viewers more individualistic in their causal attributions when the news was directed at either white crime or the criminal justice process. Episodic framing of crime also dramatically reduced references to societal treatment responsibility when the news focused on black crime. All told, however, the distinction between thematic and episodic framing proved less substantial than the particular subject matter focus of news reports in shaping attribution of responsibility for crime. Given that crime is both a highly threatening and emotionally charged issue (34 percent of the participants in this study spontaneously named crime as among the most important problems facing the country), it is remarkable that relatively modest amounts of exposure to news about illegal drugs, white or black crime, and the criminal justice process proved sufficient to induce significant shifts in viewers' attributions.

FIVE

Effects of Framing on Attributions of Responsibility for Poverty, Unemployment, and Racial Inequality

Some of the most heated and divisive conflicts in American political life have centered on issues concerning the distribution of wealth and social welfare. Today, Americans disagree over the adequacy of the government's "safety net" for the poor and the use of racial quotas in employment decisions. In the past they disagreed over the right of workers to organize and the question of slavery.

The continued prominence of social welfare issues on the national agenda is generally traced to built-in tensions between economic individualism and political egalitarianism, which have produced considerable ambivalence about poverty, economic inequality, and related issues. The presence of significant antiegalitarian strands of thought in popular culture is among the factors held to perpetuate poverty and inequality in America.[1]

The relevance of deeply rooted cultural values to attributions of responsibility for social welfare issues should render these issues stringent tests of framing. In other words, if the mainstream beliefs in the work ethic, self-reliance, and related themes constitute "dispositional" cues that encourage Americans to "blame the victims" of poverty, unemployment, or racial inequality, attributions of causal and treatment responsibility for these issues should be relatively impervious to short-term contextual cues such as media framing.[2]

This chapter describes the results of five experiments in which television news framing of poverty, unemployment, and racial inequality was manipulated. The experimental results show that attributions of responsibility for poverty and racial inequality, but not for unemployment, were subject to significant framing effects. Before proceeding to the experimental results, however, let us first examine the extent of thematic and episodic framing in network news coverage of the three issues.

How Television News Frames Poverty, Unemployment, and Racial Inequality

In comparison with crime and terrorism, the networks devoted relatively little attention to poverty, unemployment, and racial inequality. During the six-year period under examination, the networks aired more than three hundred stories on both unemployment and racial inequality and fewer than two hundred stories on poverty. Thus, the viewer of a particular network's national newscasts watched, on average, less than one story a month on poverty and between one and two stories a month on both unemployment and racial inequality.

The extent of episodic and thematic framing of each of these issues is shown in figure 5.1. As noted in chapter 3, the classification of these stories was based on the amount of news text presented in either frame; stories were classified as thematic if the thematic frame took up more text (words) in the *Abstracts* than did the episodic frame, and vice versa (see appendix A).

Unlike network coverage of crime and terrorism, which was predominantly episodic, coverage of the social welfare issues under investigation was mixed. Poverty was the only social welfare issue in

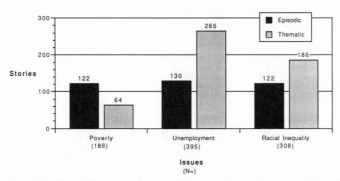

Fig. 5.1 Episodic and Thematic Coverage of Poverty, Unemployment, and Racial Inequality, 1981–86

which the expected dominance of episodic over thematic framing was observed. Episodic framing accounted for 66 percent of all coverage of poverty. In probabilistic terms, a typical viewer of network news over the six-year period would have been nearly twice as likely to encounter news about a particular instance of a poor person as news about poverty as a general issue. Following the anchor's lead-in comments, the typical story on poverty turned immediately to a close-up look at a person or persons living in poverty.

Coverage of unemployment was primarily thematic; thematic stories outnumbered episodic stories by a ratio of two to one. The typical news story on unemployment reported the release of the latest unemployment figures and consisted of interviews with economists, businessmen, or public officials who commented on the meaning of the unemployment data and the potential impact of unemployment on economic activity.

News coverage bearing on racial inequality proved considerably more complex and multifaceted than coverage of either poverty of unemployment. The content analysis revealed three major subject matter subcategories: racial discrimination, affirmative action, and economic inequality. News stories bearing on subjects with only limited relevance to racial inequality (such as reports on racial violence, blacks running for public office, and U.S. policy toward South Africa) were excluded from the analysis. Overall, thematic news stories on matters of racial inequality outnumbered episodic stories by a slight margin.

Within the issue of racial inequality, stories on discrimination accounted for nearly 70 percent of all coverage. These stories consisted primarily of reports on segregation in education and housing, employment discrimination, or voting rights infringements and the actions (or inactions) of governmental and nongovernmental entities to combat discrimination. Reports on a Supreme Court decision, disputes between Congress and the president over civil rights policy, and the changing political strategies of civil rights organizations are illustrations of thematic framing of discrimination. Reports on particular instances of discrimination (for example, Miami's segregated public schools) or stories about particular participants in the civil rights movement (for example, a story describing the reunion of blacks who organized the lunch counter sit-ins in the sixties) are illustrations of episodic framing of discrimination. News coverage of discrimination featured both thematic and episodic framing with a tilt in the direction of the former.

The remaining stories on racial inequality covered affirmative action and racial disparities in economic status. Stories on affirmative action (which accounted for only 15 percent of the total coverage), though logically a subset of discrimination coverage, were categorized separately because of their specific focus on preferential treatment for minorities through the application of either racial quotas or reverse discrimination.[3] Virtually all coverage of affirmative action was thematic and focused on judicial outcomes such as a recent Supreme Court decision limiting the use of racial employment quotas. When affirmative action was framed in episodic terms, the reports invariably described the participants in particular disputes (for example, a report on demands made by blacks in the New York City police force that race be taken into account in making promotion decisions).

In addition to reports on discrimination and affirmative action, the networks depicted economic inequalities between blacks and whites. These stories described differences between blacks and whites in terms of income, housing, education, and health. This was the most episodic of the three subject matter categories, and episodic framing made up 43 percent of all the stories.

Thus, for this time period and set of issues, poverty was the only case for which episodic framing predominated. The marked difference in the networks' framing of poverty on the one hand, and unemployment and racial inequality on the other, may be attributed to several factors. Unemployment is the most extensively recorded of the three issues; the federal government releases a barrage of employment-related numbers each month. In fact, the announcement of the monthly unemployment figures has become a routine news event. Although poverty is also presumably amenable to similar statistical updating, it has not been the focus of equivalent governmental (and hence media) attention. Moreover, current economic theory posits that levels of unemployment are key indicators of the health of the national economy, but the poverty numbers are seldom viewed in the same way. Apparently, the presumed "macro" effects of unemployment induce the networks to provide thematic rather than episodic coverage of the issue.[4]

News coverage of racial inequality is more thematic than coverage of poverty because much of the former emanates from Washington. Reports on court cases, civil rights legislation, and the "politics" of civil rights take up a large share of the coverage, and these stories are by nature thematic. In addition, the networks may avoid close-up episodic coverage of poor blacks so as to avoid charges of racial bias in the news.

Who Is Responsible?

Before taking up the framing experiments, it is helpful to compare attribution of responsibility across the three issues (see fig. 5.2). Far from being mystified by the questions probing causal and treatment responsibility, participants produced abundant spontaneous responses. The average number of causal responses was 2.3 for poverty, 2.2 for racial inequality, and 2.0 for unemployment. References to treatment responsibility were somewhat less forthcoming: poverty, racial inequality, and unemployment elicited an average of 2.1, 1.9, and 1.6 responses respectively.[5]

Following the pattern set by crime and terrorism, causal responsibility for all three issues was either assigned to individuals or to general societal factors. Individual responsibility included the themes of character deficiencies (such as laziness or immorality) and inadequate skills or education. Societal responsibility included the themes of economic conditions (such the cost of living, technological progress, and foreign trade), institutional barriers (such as racism and public apathy), and inadequate governmental efforts (such as budget cuts in social welfare programs, the ideology of the Reagan administration, and fiscal or monetary policy).[6] Finally, in the case of racial inequality, a very small fraction of responses viewed whites as in fact the "less equal" of the races and cited excess governmental protection of minorities as a causal factor.

In the area of causal attribution, poverty and unemployment were both characterized by high levels of societal responsibility. Beneath this surface resemblance, however, the issues differed in the prominence of particular societal causes. Unemployment was seen primarily as a problem created by prevailing economic circumstances. Fifty percent of all causal attributions cited broad economic forces such as rising interest rates, higher labor costs, cheaper imports, and union-management conflicts.[7] Poverty, on the other hand, was seen as caused by ineffective or inappropriate welfare programs *and* by economic circumstances. In terms of causal responsibility, therefore, poverty was more politicized than unemployment.

Racial inequality deviated markedly from both unemployment and poverty in the assignment of causal responsibility. Individuals were

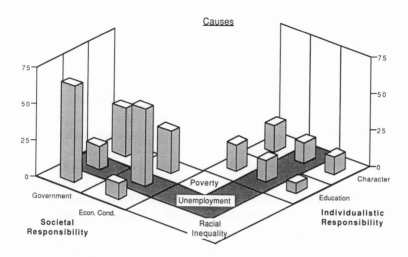

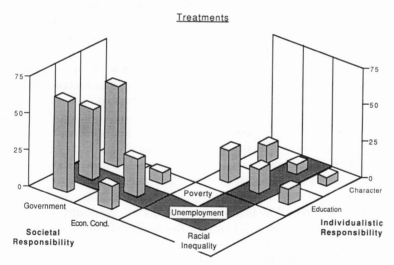

Fig. 5.2 Causal and Treatment Attribution of Responsibility for Poverty, Unemployment, and Racial Inequality

held responsible in only 19 percent of the causal responses, while institutional barriers and the lack of governmental responsiveness were held responsible in 66 percent of all responses. Cumulatively, societal responses accounted for nearly 80 percent of all causal attributions of racial inequality. Compared with poor people and the unemployed, minorities were far more likely to be seen as victims of societal or cultural forces.[8]

While the distribution of treatment attributions for crime and terrorism included few references to individualistic responsibility, participants' treatment suggestions for the social welfare issues *were* directed at actions by individuals (individualistic responsibility), such as hard work and the acquisition of job skills, as well as at actions by government and society (societal responsibility), including lowered institutional barriers to economic mobility and strengthened or improved governmental efforts. Economic changes cited included lowering interest rates, creating unskilled jobs, and so on. In the case of racial inequality, a small fraction of treatment responses called specifically for ending governmental favoritism toward minorities.

Treatment attributions for both racial inequality and unemployment were overwhelmingly societal. Both issues diverged sharply from poverty, where the mix of societal and individual treatment responsibility was more balanced. In comparison with the unemployed and members of minority groups, the poor were perceived as having greater control over their fate.

It is instructive to assess the pattern of convergence between causal and treatment responsibility. For this purpose a dichotomized "net" causal and treatment responsibility score was computed for each issue; low scorers had a relatively strong sense of individualistic causal (or treatment) responsibility and high scorers have a relatively strong sense of societal causal (or treatment) responsibility (see appendix B).

Using this approach, there were four possible combinations of causal and treatment responsibility for racial inequality, unemployment, and poverty. Following research by Brickman and his associates, these combinations were labelled as follows:

1. *Societal model:* societal conditions cause the problem; societal efforts are the treatment.
2. *Individual model:* individuals are responsible for both cause and treatment.
3. *Guardianship model:* individuals are causally responsible; society is responsible for treatment.
4. *Compensatory model:* to compensate for handicaps imposed by society, individuals must extend increased effort.[9]

The interdependence of causal and treatment responsibility for the three issues is shown in figure 5.3. The prominence of the four mod-

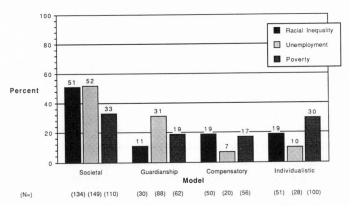

Fig. 5.3   Models of Responsibility: Poverty, Racial Inequality, and Unemployment

els varied considerably with the issue. The societal model dominated in the cases of racial inequality and unemployment, where more respondents fell into this cell (51 and 52 percent, respectively) than in all other cells combined. The societal model was weakest (33 percent) in the case of poverty. At the opposite extreme, the individualistic model was applied most frequently to poverty and least frequently to unemployment. The guardianship model was most significant in the case of unemployment (31 percent). Finally, the compensatory model applied to virtually no respondents when unemployment was the target issue and to less than 20 percent of the sample when poverty and racial inequality were considered.

Attributions of causal and treatment responsibility corresponded in all three issue areas, though the degree of overlap was far from perfect. The correspondence was highest for racial inequality where 70 percent of the sample expressed consistent causal and treatment attributions. The comparable figures for poverty and unemployment were 66 and 63 percent, respectively.

Experimental Tests of Framing

Poverty Experiment 1

This study established five experimental conditions. Two presented poverty within a thematic news frame, while the remaining three provided viewers with episodic coverage. In the first condition, "National Poverty," participants watched a news report that documented both the increase in poverty nationwide since 1980 and the significant reductions in the scope of federal social welfare programs. In the second condition, "High Unemployment," participants watched a story that juxtaposed the national unemployment rate and the size of the federal budget deficit. Both of these conditions epitomized the thematic frame; poverty was depicted in terms of collective or societal outcomes and trends.

The three remaining conditions framed poverty in terms of particular episodes or victims of economic hardship. The first episodic report, "High cost of Heat," described unusually harsh winter weather in the upper Midwest and portrayed two families unable to pay their heating bills. The second condition, "Homeless," focused on homeless individuals—two black teenagers living in the streets of New York City and a white couple forced to live in their car in San Diego.[10] Finally, the third episodic condition, "Unemployed Worker," described the financial difficulties facing the family of an unemployed auto worker in Ohio.

In order to examine framing effects on causal and treatment attributions, indices of societal and individualistic responsibility were computed corresponding to the number of societal or individualistic responses divided by the total number of responses. In the case of individualistic causal responsibility, for example, the index was the percentage of causal responses citing character or education (see appendix B). As the initial test of framing, the results in the combined thematic framing conditions were compared with the pattern elicited by the combined episodic framing conditions (fig. 5.4).

The effects of framing proved robust in the area of causal attributions. Individualistic attributions for poverty were more than twice as prominent under conditions of episodic framing. Conversely, the frequency of societal causal attributions was substantially higher following exposure to thematic framing of poverty. Framing effects on attributions of treatment responsibility were much less striking. Although the episodic reports elicited noticeably more individualistic treatment attributions, references to societal treatment responsibility were unaffected by framing.

The aggregated results shown in figure 5.4 represent the least stringent test of framing because they ignore potential differences in the impact of particular news stories. The next step of the analysis assessed the effects of the individual episodic and thematic conditions on attributions of responsibility (fig. 5.5).

The direction in which participants assigned causal responsibility

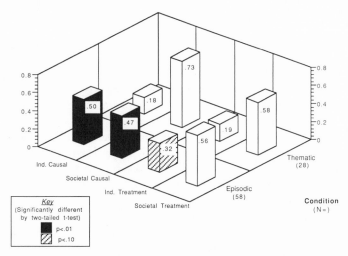

Fig. 5.4 Framing Effects (Aggregated): Poverty Experiment 1

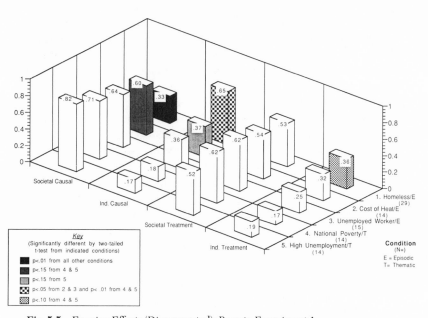

Fig. 5.5 Framing Effects (Disaggregated): Poverty Experiment 1

was significantly altered in both the thematic and the Homeless conditions. After watching accounts of homeless people, the experimental participants were especially drawn to the character and education of poor people as the causes of poverty. After watching thematic framing of both poverty and unemployment, causal responsibility was assigned to society rather than individuals by a margin of greater than four to one. The index of societal responsibility ranged from .33 in the Homeless condition (which differed significantly from all other conditions) to .82 in the High Unemployment condition (which also differed marginally from the High Cost of Heat condition). Conversely, the index of individualistic causal responsibility was highest in the Homeless condition (again significantly different from all other conditions) and lowest in the High Unemployment condition. Although the High Cost of Heat condition elicited significantly fewer responses to individualistic causal responsibility than the Homeless condition, the level of individualistic responsibility in the former was significantly higher than the comparable level in both thematic conditions.

As the difference between the Homeless and the High Cost of Heat conditions indicated, framing poverty in episodic terms did not consistently evoke individualistic causal attributions. The homeless person, the unemployed worker, and the family unable to pay its heating bill all represent people facing economic adversity, yet they elicited noticeably divergent explanations of poverty. Homeless people were significantly more likely than either people unable to pay their heating bills or unemployed workers to elicit attributions of individualistic causal responsibility. In short, whereas the homeless elicited a predominantly individualistic sense of causal responsibility, unemployed workers and individuals unable to meet their heating bills elicited a relatively high level of societal causal responsibility.

News coverage of homeless people may encourage viewers to hold poor people responsible more frequently because the homeless fit our mental representations of "poor people" more closely than unemployed workers or families living in unheated homes. Alternatively, it may be that the homeless, lacking even a roof over their heads, embody a particularly extreme form of economic adversity. There is evidence in the psychological literature on causal attribution that more extreme outcomes prompt a stronger sense of individualistic responsibility.[11] Because the homeless have apparently lost everything, people reason that there must be something deficient in their character; if not, homelessness could happen to "ordinary people," a rather threatening proposition.[12]

Framing effects were negligible in the area of treatment responsibility. While both thematic framing conditions triggered the highest proportion of societal treatment responses, participants in all five experimental conditions were more prone to assign society (rather than poor people) the responsibility for treating poverty. The Homeless condition was once again characterized by the most developed sense of individualistic treatment responsibility among the three episodic framing conditions, followed by the Unemployed Worker and the High Cost of Heat conditions.

All told, the results from Experiment 1 suggest that the direction in which individuals assign responsibility for poverty varies with the particular frame they encounter in the evening news. When network news reports on poverty thematically, viewers tend to attribute responsibility to societal agents of institutions; when the networks report on poverty in episodic terms, viewers tend to attribute responsibility to the poor themselves; however, episodic reports elicit varying degrees of societal and individualistic responsibility, depending upon the type of poor person depicted.

Poverty Experiment 2

This study was designed to replicate and elaborate upon the results of the first experiment. Thirteen experimental conditions were established. Three separate conditions presented the thematic frame: "Rising Unemployment" (a report detailing difficulties facing the manufacturing sector), "Rising Poverty" (a story reporting increases in the number of Americans meeting the government's definition of poverty), and "Hunger in America" (a report on a Harvard University study showing significant increases in the number of American households requiring emergency food aid). The three thematic framing conditions proved equivalent in that there was not one significant difference between them in either attribution of causal or treatment responsibility; the responses to these conditions were therefore pooled.

Because the results from the first experiment suggested that particular qualities of poor people may affect attributions for poverty, the episodic framing manipulation in this experiment was made more elaborate to include five categories of poor people. Participants either watched an unemployed male, an adult single mother, an elderly widow, a young child, or a teenage single mother describe their economic difficulties. These five groups account for most Americans receiving public assistance.[13] Each of these five victim groups was presented in two versions, with the race of the individual being either black or white. The purpose here was to replicate the results from the experiment on crime and to assess whether episodic framing and viewers' racial stereotypes jointly influence individuals' understanding of poverty (see appendix B). Unlike the first experiment, the general level of visible economic distress was held roughly constant across all the episodic framing conditions; thus all the poor people depicted in the news stories had access to modest housing, appeared reasonably well clothed and healthy, and so on. In short, the individual victims did not differ markedly in the severity of their poverty. The differences in causal and treatment responsibility between the pooled thematic framing conditions and the separate episodic conditions are shown in figure 5.6.[14]

As in Experiment 1, participants were generally least apt to hold

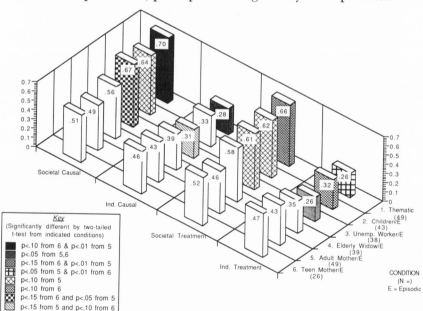

Fig. 5.6 Framing Effects: Poverty Experiment 2

individuals causally responsible and most apt to consider society responsible when the news was framed thematically. The mean index of societal causal responsibility reached .70 in the pooled thematic conditions, which differed significantly from the Adult Single Mother and Teenage Single Mother episodic conditions. Also in keeping with Experiment 1, there were significant differences among the various episodic conditions. Single mothers elicited a particularly high level of individualistic causal attributions and differed significantly from young children and unemployed men who tended to elicit primarily societal causal attributions.

Similar framing effects were obtained in the area of treatment responsibility. In general, participants in all conditions were as willing to assign society the responsibility for treating poverty as they were to consider society causally responsible. The two single-mother conditions, however, pulled the highest proportion of individualistic treatment attributions and, correspondingly, the lowest proportion of societal treatment attributions. In both respects episodic framing of single mothers deviated significantly from thematic framing. The single-mother conditions also differed, though to a lesser degree, from the episodic conditions featuring young children and unemployed men.

The analysis next considered the effects of the poor person's race on viewers' attributions. The indices of societal and individualistic responsibility were subjected to a five-by-two analysis of variance (corresponding to the five categories of poor people and the two races). (See figure 5.7).

Race provided only a weak cue for attributions of causal responsibility. The main effects of race on the frequency of individualistic and societal causes were not significant, but there were very faint traces of racial differences for the latter: black poor people were, by the slightest of margins, less likely than whites to elicit societal causes $(F_{race} = 1.29, p < .25)$.

More pronounced racial differences emerged in the area of treatment attributions. Regardless of condition, black poor people elicited more individualistic attributions $(F_{race} < .05)$ and fewer societal attributions $(F_{race} < .10)$. Within this general pattern, the racial differences were most prominent for adult single mothers; in comparison with the white mother, the black mother elicited twice the proportion of individualistic treatment attributions. In short, the de-

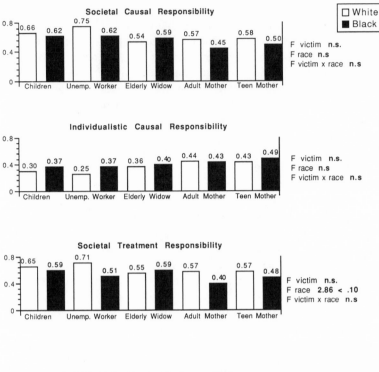

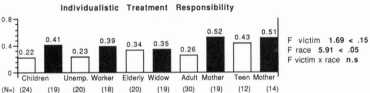

Fig. 5.7 Individual-Victim and Racial Differences in Attribution of Causal and Treatment Responsibility: Poverty Experiment 2

gree to which societal intervention was considered an appropriate remedy for poverty was lessened when the poor person depicted was black.

Experiments 1 and 2 thus suggest that television news presentations do affect what people identify as the causes and cures of poverty, and this effect is achieved through variations in framing. When poverty is defined thematically, responsibility tends to be assigned differently then when poverty is defined episodically, in terms of specific instances of poor people. People hold the government responsible to a greater degree when the news frame is thematic. In addition to the distinction between thematic and episodic framing, different categories of victims elicit different patterns of responsibility. Elderly widows, children, and unemployed males are seen as "needy;" single mothers (both adults and teenagers) are seen as less "deserving." Finally, the race of the poor person is a meaningful cue when people think about poverty. Black poverty tends to be understood in terms of individualistic treatment responsibility; white poverty is understood in terms of societal treatment responsibility.

Unemployment Experiment 1

Because news coverage of unemployment is heavily thematic, two of the three conditions in this study—"High Unemployment" and "Economics of Steel"—were devoted to the thematic frame The High Unemployment condition, which described trends in the national unemployment figures and the federal budget deficit, featured the same report used in Poverty Experiment 1. The Economics of Steel condition described the various difficulties facing U.S. steel companies, including high labor costs, outdated and inefficient physical plants, and subsidized foreign competitors. The episodic framing condition, "Unemployed Worker," was also taken from Poverty Experiment 1 and described the travails of an unemployed auto worker. (See figure 5.8.)

The overwhelming attribution of causal and treatment responsibility for unemployment to societal factors was simply unaffected by news coverage. Within the category of societal responsibility, the great majority of attributions in all three conditions referred to current economic circumstances. Treatment responsibility was extensively attributed to society (76 percent of all responses) even when viewers were confronted with the episodic frame. Interestingly, when this story was used as the episodic frame for poverty, it elicited a much higher level of individualistic attributions.

Unemployment Experiment 2

As a second test of framing, three new conditions were constructed, one thematic and two episodic. The thematic condition featured a news report on the state of unemployment nationwide and

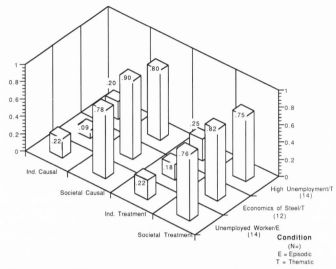

Fig. 5.8 Framing Effects: Unemployment Experiment 1

differences between particular regions in employment trends. The two episodic conditions presented coverage of an unemployed male workers. In one condition the worker was black, and in the other he was white. (Both of these news reports were taken from the second poverty experiment.) This manipulation, which was suggested by the results in the second poverty experiment, was designed to ascertain the degree to which racial stereotypes affect attributions of responsibility. (See figure 5.9.)

Again, no statistically significant framing effects were observed, and societal factors were cited for both causal and treatment responsibility. Once again, the overwhelming majority of societal attributions referred to the state of the economy. Attribution of responsibility for unemployment was thus unaffected by the frame employed in television news coverage.

It is possible that the absence of detectable media influence on attributions of responsibility for unemployment stems from the sustained prominence of the economy in the nation's political discourse. That is, the continued high salience of *national* economic problems may have cued individuals to think of "the economy" as a catchall locus of responsibility. Alternatively, the term "unemployment" may itself represent a "semantic frame," or wording effect, that directs individuals to think of the issue as a collective rather than individual outcome. Asking people, "Why are so many Americans out of work?" may elicit more societal-oriented responses than asking, "Why did John Smith lose his job?"

Racial Inequality Experiment 1

The three major subject categories revealed in the content analysis were examined in three experimental manipulations: "Racial Discrimination," "Black Poverty," and "Affirmative Action." Coverage of discrimination was presented only in the thematic frame. Coverage of black poverty and affirmative action appeared in both the thematic and episodic frames.

Participants assigned to the Racial Discrimination condition watched a news story that described the results of a study in which the performance of black pupils in the Connecticut public schools was tracked before and after implementation of desegregation programs. The report noted the marked improvement in black students' grades, college entrance-exam scores, and job prospects following desegregation.

The news story used in the "Affirmative Action–Thematic" condition described the evolution of preferential employment policy in the United States and explained the Supreme Court's reasoning in a recent decision upholding the constitutionality of preferential treat-

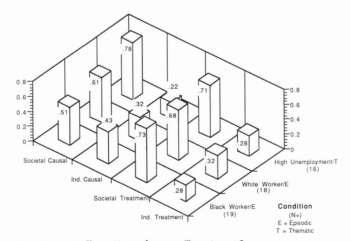

Fig. 5.9 Framing Effects: Unemployment Experiment 2

ment for racial minorities. The news story used in the "Affirmative Action–Episodic" condition reported on a Cleveland fire fighting unit that had been ordered to promote black fire fighters ahead of whites. Black and white fire fighters were interviewed, the former supporting the action and the latter condemning it. The two affirmative action stories thus differed only in their specificity: viewers watched either news coverage of affirmative action as general public policy or news coverage of a particular employment dispute.

Three news conditions on black poverty, one thematic and two episodic, were constructed. The story used in the "Black Poverty–Thematic" condition was an account of black-white disparities in various standard of living indicators. Two episodic conditions were used in order to determine whether personal characteristics would affect attributions for racial inequality. The poor person in one story ("Unemployed Worker") was an unemployed male and in the other ("Teenage Single Mother") was an unmarried teenage mother. Both stories were also used in the second experiment on poverty.

There were several expectations underlying this design. First, the general framing hypothesis suggests that episodic framing should elicit a stronger sense of individualistic responsibility for racial inequality than would thematic framing. Second, because the experimental data revealed high levels of individualistic attributions for poverty (relative to unemployment and racial inequality), news coverage of black poverty was expected to enhance individualistic attributions of responsibility for this manifestation of racial inequality. Third, news coverage of discrimination, by drawing attention to societal handicaps imposed on minorities (such as school segregation), was expected to suggest societal responsibility, while coverage of affirmative action was expected to provoke some backlash among the predominantly white participants in the form of a lessened sense of societal responsibility.

To analyze the effects of the framing and subject matter manipulations, composite indices of individual and societal responsibility were computed for each participant. The indices of individualistic causal and treatment responsibility were the proportion of attributions citing character and education. The indices of societal causal and treatment responsibility were the proportion of attributions citing societal factors (see appendix B). In addition to individualistic and societal responsibility, the analysis also investigated differences in viewers' tendency to cite causes and treatments referring to "excess" affirmative action and reverse discrimination.

The first stage of the analysis investigated differences within the affirmative action manipulation between the thematic and episodic conditions and within the black poverty manipulation between the thematic and the two episodic conditions. Contrary to expectations, thematic and episodic framing of affirmative action elicited an identical pattern of responses. These conditions were therefore combined. The two conditions representing episodic framing of black poverty also proved equivalent and were similarly combined. The experimental design for racial inequality was thus reduced to four conditions: Affirmative Action, Racial Discrimination, Black Poverty –Thematic, and Black Poverty–Episodic. (See figure 5.10.)

Of these four conditions, the Black Poverty–Episodic condition elicited the highest frequency (42 percent) of individualistic attributions. This was consistent with the expectation that individualistic attributions would be triggered both because the news story appeared in the episodic frame and because the story touched on poverty, which had already been determined to produce relatively high levels of individualistic attributions regardless of frame. In the remaining conditions, societal attributions outweighed individualistic attributions by a factor of at least three to one. The Black

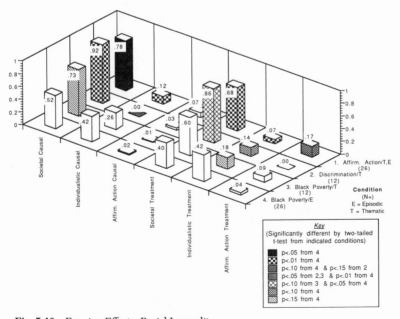

Fig. 5.10   Framing Effects: Racial Inequality

Poverty–Episodic condition elicited significantly higher levels of individualistic treatment responsibility than all remaining conditions and significantly higher levels of individual causal responsibility than the Racial Discrimination and Affirmative Action conditions. In short, providing viewers with information about a poor black person prompted a relative outpouring of individualistic attributions for racial inequality.

While episodic framing of black poverty provoked individualistic attributions, thematic framing of racial discrimination had precisely the opposite effect. After exposure to the news report on school desegregation, virtually every causal attribution for racial inequality concerned society. Not once did individuals assigned to the Racial Discrimination condition refer to character or education as relevant causal factors, a result that differed significantly from all other conditions. A similarly lopsided distribution prevailed for treatment attributions; some 90 percent of the prescribed cures in the Racial Discrimination condition addressed societal responses to racial inequality.

News coverage of affirmative action influenced attributions of causal and treatment responsibility for racial inequality, but without regard to frame. Responses referring to affirmative action policy itself as a cause of racial inequality peaked in the Affirmative Action conditions. Watching news accounts of affirmative action prompted a few respondents to deny that black suffer from inequality. Similarly, the proportion of treatment attributions calling for an end to affirmative action was highest in this condition, a result that differed significantly from the Racial Discrimination and Black Poverty–Episodic conditions.

Thus, the overall pattern of results for racial inequality suggests that framing and the subject matter focus of the news both influence attributions. When television news covered racial discrimination in thematic terms, viewers gave predominantly societal attributions for racial inequality. When viewers' attention was drawn to preferential treatment of minorities, the locus of responsibility was still predominantly societal, but disapproving references to governmental favoritism were more prominent, as were treatment prescriptions of an end to official favoritism. When the news covered black poverty in thematic terms, although societal attributions for racial inequality again dominated, references to individualistic responsibility increased substantially. Finally, when black poverty was framed in episodic terms, individualistic and societal responsibility were equally prominent.

Conclusion

Taken together, the five experiments indicate that network news stories can affect how people attribute responsibility for poverty and racial inequality. Episodic framing of poverty increased attributions of individualistic responsibility, while thematic framing increased attributions of societal responsibility. News coverage of different types of poor people may raise or lower societal attributions depending on the personal characteristics of the poor person depicted. News coverage of black poverty in general and episodic coverage of black poverty in particular increases the degree to which viewers hold individuals responsible for racial inequality. News coverage of racial discrimination has the opposite effect. Attribution of responsibility for unemployment, however, is unaffected by the manner in which the networks frame the issue. Citizens understand unemployment primarily in economic terms under conditions of both thematic and episodic framing.

When placed in the context of actual network coverage, the experimental results suggest that the predominant news frame for poverty has the effect of shifting responsibility from society to the poor. Were the networks to increase the level of thematic framing in their coverage of poverty, Americans might be more apt to consider society or government rather than the poor responsible. The prevailing direction of network news coverage of racial inequality—racial discrimination—has the opposite effect, namely, that of increasing societal attributions. When news editors decide to present stories on black poverty, however, the effect may be to shift responsibility from society to poor blacks.

The experimental results are especially striking given that both poverty and racial inequality are closely intertwined with mainstream American values. As noted at the outset of this chapter, cultural values are among the factors held to perpetuate poverty. The results reported here indicate, however, that the well-documented tendency of Americans to consider poor people responsible may be due not only to dominant cultural values but also to news coverage of poverty in which images of poor people predominate.

Race is itself a meaningful contextual cue when people think about poverty. Our sample of white, middle-class Americans were sensitive to skin color, depending upon the type of poor person depicted. Like race, a poor person's gender also appears to activate a more individualistic-and less societal-oriented conception of responsibility for poverty. Whether gender per se is the critical cue is not known since viewers in the framing experiments were not provided coverage of an unemployed woman, male retiree, or single male parent. What the evidence does indicate is that single mothers elicit a "blaming the victim" syndrome; they are considered particularly responsible for their economic circumstances and less deserving of governmental support. Finally, the particular combination of race, gender, age, and marital status (that is, black adult single mothers) was particularly evocative of individualistic responsibility for poverty. This particular demographic combination represents the largest segment of poor adults in America. In this sense, the most "realistic" episodic news frame had the most inhibiting effect on societal attributions of responsibility.

SIX

Effects of Framing on Attributions of Responsibility for the Iran-Contra Affair

The various tests of network framing reported thus far concern long-standing social and political issues. In this chapter, the analysis of network framing is extended to attributions of responsibility for a specific decision by the executive branch of government, namely, the decision to sell arms to the Iranians. Because responsibility for the Iran arms sale was obviously purely governmental, framing is tested in this case by examining the degree to which alternative news frames induced viewers to attribute the decision either to President Reagan or to situational pressures such as the escalating tensions in the Middle East.

The revelation that the Reagan administration had been secretly supplying arms to the regime of Ayatollah Khomeini sent political shock waves throughout the world. The ensuing events and crescendo of media coverage proved that not even Ronald Reagan's buoyant public image could withstand a steady barrage of bad news. Despite the president's repeated assertions of ignorance and the Tower Commission's having absolved him of direct or indirect complicity in the operation, many Americans found it difficult to believe that the president was completely "out of the loop." In November 1986, for instance, shortly after the media broke the story, 50 percent of the public responded yes to the question, "Do you think that Ronald Reagan knew that money from the Iranian arms sales was going to help the Contras in Nicaragua?" In this same survey (conducted jointly by the *New York Times* and "CBS News"), when asked, "Whether or not Ronald Reagan knew about the money being sent to the Contras, how much do you hold him responsible for it?" 56 percent of the public responded, "A lot."

The facts of the Iran arms sale and the extent to which the American public held their president responsible are particularly relevant to research on presidential popularity. Since the 1940s, pollsters have regularly recorded the incumbent president's popularity by asking Americans whether they approve or disapprove "of the way president _____ is handling his job as president." The degree of presidential popularity is widely regarded as a critical diagnostic indicator of the president's capacity to lead; the higher the level of popularity, the greater the effectiveness of the president's legislative and other policy-making initiatives.[1]

Under the most widely accepted theory of presidential popularity, citizens' evaluations of the president depend upon the state of the national economy and other salient political events such as international summit conferences, domestic scandals, and military conflicts. Ostrom and Simon, for example, have differentiated between "approval-enhancing" and "approval-diminishing" events. The former include international crises and dramatic events (for example, the *Challenger* disaster and the invasion of Grenada) that unify the public behind the president. The latter consist primarily of incidents of corruption or wrongdoing within the administration, the implementation of policies that evoke widespread controversy, and dramatic indications of economic weakness, such as the stock market crash of 1987.[2]

The Iran-Contra affair was clearly an approval-diminishing event. Analyses of President Reagan's popularity have demonstrated that as the American public learned of the administration's sale of arms to Iran, and in the growing political controversy in the aftermath of the disclosure, their evaluations of the president became significantly less positive. In fact, the effects of the Iran-Contra affair on President Reagan's popularity were comparable to the effects of the Watergate scandal on President Nixon's popularity.[3]

The proven impact of all sorts of political events on presidential popularity indicates that Americans attribute responsibility (either causal or treatment) for these events to the president. The imputation of responsibility to the president is consistent with attribution theory, which suggests that people typically emphasize the role of individual actions and intentions when attributing causal responsibility for events, while simultaneously discounting the effects of impersonal, situational forces.[4] According to this research, the great majority of Americans could be expected to explain the administration's decision to provide arms to Iran primarily by perceived motives, traits, or other characteristics of their leaders, particularly their president. This prediction, however, rests on the assumption that people attempt to make sense of complex events dispassionately, simply on the basis of what they observe. In the case of the Iran arms sale, however, attributions of responsibility are likely to be colored by partisan biases. Supporters of President Reagan had good reason to ignore the effects of his actions or traits, while opponents were particularly likely to seize upon the president's leadership as a principal causal factor. More generally, friends and foes of the president were expected to engage in "defensive attribution" thus making the behavior or character of the president factors of variable importance in attributions of responsibility for the arms sale.

Regardless of the question of partisan bias, if people tend to attribute responsibility for political events to the president, and if these attributions affect the public's approval or disapproval of the president, then network framing of events is clearly relevant to the analysis of presidential popularity. The Iran-Contra experiment was designed to investigate whether the same event could be either approval-enhancing or approval-diminishing, depending upon the perspective provided by the news. Before proceeding to the design of the experiment, however, it is necessary to describe the results of the content analysis of the networks' coverage of the Iran-Contra affair.

How the Networks Covered the Iran-Contra Affair

The disclosure that the Reagan administration had secretly supplied arms and equipment to Iran, and the ensuing events, captured the full attention of the networks. Between November 1986 and September 1987, ABC, CBS, and NBC broadcast more than twelve hundred reports (which represented more than sixty hours of airtime) bearing on these events. Since the sale of arms to Iran and the resulting effort to "refinance" the Contras were specific governmental decisions (rather than on ongoing government policy) news reports about these decisions typically focused on daily events, statements, or press briefings. Since virtually all reports were episodic, the distinction between thematic and episodic framing is of little relevance to news coverage of the Iran-Contra affair. The content analysis revealed, however, that the networks consistently employed either of two frameworks when reporting Iran-Contra news—events were either portrayed in the context of foreign policy objectives or as the source of political controversy.

Nearly 70 percent of news reports cast Iran-Contra events against a backdrop of rising political controversy (see figure 6.1). Representative of "political framing" were news stories that showed Democratic (and some Republican) members of Congress condemning the decision, described the turmoil and infighting within the inner reaches of the Reagan administration, or provided critical analyses of President Reagan's leadership style and reports on the potential political fallout from the controversy for the 1988 presidential campaign.

Political framing of Iran-Contra developments included two subcategories. One set of political reports bore directly on questions of presidential leadership (including the president's efforts to cope with the crisis and his relations with his advisors). These reports were negative in tone and conveyed an impression of disarray at the White House: the president had either been unaware of his administration's actions or he knowingly participated in subverting and breaking the law. The second (and slightly more frequent) form of political framing consisted of more "objective" reports that were neutral in tone and described the flow of daily events (such as stories covering testimony given before the Joint Committee and stories describing the role of particular individuals in the covert operations).

In addition to the dominant political news frame, the networks also covered Iran-Contra events with a more programmatic or instrumental perspective. Stories in this "policy frame" transferred viewers'

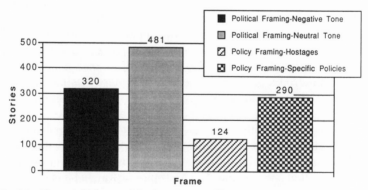

Fig. 6.1 Network Coverage of the Iran-Contra Affair

attention from questions of inadequate presidential leadership to political situations in the Middle East and the administration's efforts to respond to these situations. These reports dealt chiefly with American hostages in Lebanon and political conflicts in the Middle East. Reports on the hostages consisted typically of announcements and communiqués from the terrorist groups holding the hostages and reactions from the hostages' families and spokespersons for the administration. Hostage-related stories made up the smallest subset (10 percent) of Iran-Contra coverage. Stories covering Middle East tensions (which accounted for 24 percent of all coverage) typically concerned the Gulf War between Iran and Iraq, U.S. counterterrorism policy, political infighting within the Iranian regime, and the state of U.S.-Iranian diplomatic relations. In effect, this type of story used the Iran-Contra affair as a timely "news peg" for reporting on the Middle East, terrorism, and related foreign policy matters.

Design of the Framing Study

While remaining faithful to the pattern of actual Iran-Contra news coverage, the framing manipulation was designed to suggest either inadequate leadership or particular foreign policy considerations as potential causes of the administration's decisions (including the sale of arms to Iran and the use of the proceeds to fund the Contras). The primary objective of the experiment was to investigate whether news coverage suggesting inadequate presidential leadership would elicit attributions of presidential responsibility, and conversely whether coverage focusing on the foreign policy background would make attributions referring to situational or contextual factors more salient.

The experiment was run in August and September of 1987, shortly after the conclusion of the Congressional Joint Committee Hearings. Since the Iran arms sale represented a specific decision that had already been taken and terminated rather than an ongoing issue or problem, participants were asked only for their attributions of causal responsibility. Specifically, they were asked, "In your opinion, why did the Reagan administration decide to sell arms to Iran?"

Five framing conditions were constructed. Two of the conditions epitomized the networks' political frame for the arms sale; this coverage dwelled on the president's actions and the controversies surrounding them. Both of these conditions featured a news report that depicted President Reagan defending his actions and denying that the arms sale represented payment of ransom for hostages. In the first report, "Can Reagan be Trusted?," the correspondent stressed the importance of an impending presidential press conference as the "most important press conference of the Reagan Presidency" and then itemized a list of inconsistencies in the administration's account of the arms sale. The report concluded with the statement that the "personal trust and credibility of the president" were at stake.

The report featured in the second condition, "Who's in Charge?," was similar, except that questions of candor and trustworthiness were replaced with questions of competence and control. The report began with the reporter noting several misstatements and contradictions during President Reagan's press conference (the same press conference referred to in the first report). Portions of the president's comments were played, and the reporter noted the unusual "clarification" issued by the White House immediately following the press conference. The report closed with an interchange between anchorperson and reporter in which the latter noted that the press conference raised serious questions as to whether President Reagan was "in command of the facts."

Thus, both of the political framing conditions focused on presidential actions and rhetoric within an ambience of rising political controversy and crisis. In the first condition, the president's behavior was interpreted as raising questions about his truthfulness and candor, while in the second condition, it was interpreted as suggestive of the president's lack of knowledge and competence. Since the political conditions focused attention on the president's deeds and words, both were expected to elicit attributions of personal presidential responsibility.

The three remaining policy framing conditions made no reference to the president or to the storm of political controversy surrounding the arms sale. In the first condition, "Arms for Hostages," the story reported the number of Americans then held hostage in Beirut and focused particularly on William Buckley, reputed to be the CIA station chief there. The reporter quoted a "high-level" source within the Israeli government who had served as an intermediary between the Americans and Iranians to the effect that the transaction was "essentially an arms-for-hostages deal, 500 TOWS for William Buckley."

The two remaining policy conditions presented the arms sale in the context of Middle East politics. In the "Gulf War" condition, the anchor introduced the story with a chronology of the conflict between

Iran and Iraq, and the report then described recent unsuccessful U.S. diplomatic efforts to mediate between the combatants. In the "U.S.-Iran relations" condition, the report provided a chronological survey of the state of U.S.-Iranian relations since the fall of the shah. Neither of these conditions explicitly linked the Iranian arms sale to developments in the Middle East; nonetheless, by using the arms sale as a "peg" for coverage of the Middle East, they directed attention to the political tensions in the region.

In short, this experiment incorporated the two major news frames for the Iran arms sale—political framing versus policy framing. In the former, the administration's sale of arms to Iran was depicted in terms of inadequate presidential leadership; in the latter the arms sale became a policy response addressed either at securing the release of American hostages, or attempting to ease the conflicts in the Middle East. Participants assigned to the political framing conditions were expected to hold the president personally responsible, while viewers assigned to the policy framing conditions were expected to attribute responsibility for the arms sale to situational pressures or policy-related motives.

Results

Participants mentioned up to four different responses when asked why the administration had sold arms to Iran. As shown in figure 6.2, participants attributions fell into two broad categories. Presidential (or dispositional) responsibility consisted of explicit references to the quality or style of the president's leadership (including his apathy and weak managerial skills), other personal traits (including his commit-

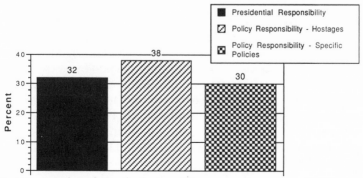

Fig. 6.2 Causal Attribution for the Arms Sale

ment to fight communism and his unwillingness to compromise with Democrats in Congress), and his consuming focus on political imagery (for example, the assertions that arms were provided to the Iranians so that the president could take credit for freeing the hostages, or that Reagan was preoccupied with questions of public relations and ignored substance).

In the great majority of presidential attributions, the presidential reference was explicit (for instance, "the president knows little about what happens in his office," or "Reagan lets his staff make the decisions"); in some cases, however, dispositional explanations were offered without directly naming the president (for example, "incompetence at the top," "stupidity," "no one in charge in Washington"). References to presidential responsibility accounted for 32 percent of all causal attributions.

Policy responsibility encompassed explanations that attributed the Iran-Contra affair to policy-based strategies or to institutional responses to particular situations rather than to individual traits. Policy-based explanations either treated the arms sale as an instrument of specific U.S. foreign policy objectives or as a means of obtaining the release of hostages. Specific policies cited included mediation of the Gulf War, improving diplomatic relations with Iran, and providing additional support for the Nicaraguan Contras and other anticommunist groups. Attributions citing specific policies represented 30 percent of the explanations. Attributions referring to the objective of releasing the hostages tended to be more diffuse (for example, "trying to pressure terrorist groups"; "they wanted the hostages out of there") and represented 38 percent of all responses.

An anticipated, Democrats and Republicans differed in their views of the arms sale. An index of presidential responsibility was constructed by calculating the percentage of causal attributions that implicated the president from which the percentage of attributions referring to policy-oriented and hostage-related considerations was subtracted. This difference score was then cut into two categories at the midpoint. High scorers were those preferring presidential over policy explanations. Fifty-six percent of the Democrats and 41 percent of the Republicans were in this group. Political ideology was associated with an even bigger difference in attributions of responsibility; 75 percent of the liberals cited presidential leadership or character, while 70 percent of the conservatives cited policy objectives.

It is difficult to compare the results from the framing experiment with national-opinion data because no national poll directly probed attributions of causal responsibility for the arms sale. As noted above, however, national surveys conducted at the time regularly asked their respondents to indicate whether they believed President Reagan knew about the arms sale and diversion of funds to the Contras. On the assumption that respondents who considered the president knowledgeable would be more likely to attribute causal responsibility to him, responses to this question were used as a rough barometer of presidential attributions. Using this indicator, the level of presidential responsibility was substantial among respondents in several "CBS News"–*New York Times* surveys administered between November 1986 and August 1987.[5] On average, a slight majority (51 percent) of the public held the president responsible (i.e., responded that he knew about the policy).[6]

One of the five "CBS News–*New York Times* polls included—in addition to the question about whether the president knew about the money going to the Contras—an open-ended question more appropriate for comparisons with the framing-study results. Respondents in the 16 July 1987 survey were asked a battery of questions concerning Colonel Oliver North's testimony at the Iran-Contra hearings. Included in this set was the question, "Do you think Oliver North lied about anything?" Respondents who indicated that North had lied were then asked the follow-up question, "What did he lie about?" Responses to this open-ended question represent a more spontaneous indicator of presidential responsibility and hence provide a more appropriate comparison point with the "most important causes" question used in the Suffolk County framing study. Twenty-five percent of the national sample stated that North had lied about the extent of President Reagan's involvement. This level of presidential responsibility was quite close to the level recorded in the framing experiment (32 percent).

The national data also further corroborated the framing-study results in demonstrating strong partisan biases in the attributions. Americans divided sharply according to their party affiliation when they responded to the question asking whether President Reagan knew about the money going to the Contras (see figure 6.3). Democrats, by an average margin in excess of two to one, were more likely than Republicans to say that the president was aware of the arms sale. Similarly, on average, 60 percent of self-identified "liberals" held the

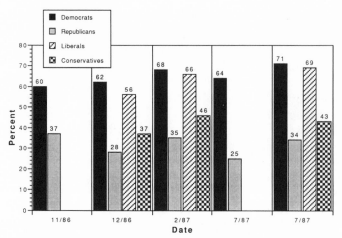

Fig. 6.3   Partisan and Ideological Bias in Attribution of Presidential Responsibility for the Arms Sale: "CBS News"–*New York Times* Surveys

president responsible; among conservatives, the level of presidential responsibility was only 42 percent.

Preliminary analyses of the experimental results established that the two political framing conditions ("Can Reagan be Trusted" and "Who's in Charge") did not differ significantly in the percentage of viewers citing personal or policy-related attributions. These conditions were therefore pooled.[7] The two conditions providing coverage of political tensions in the Middle East ("Gulf War" and "U.S.-Iran Relations") also proved identical in their effects on viewers' causal attributions, and they, too, were pooled. The design was thus reduced to three conditions: "Political Framing," "Arms for Hostages," and "Middle East Conflicts." The analysis assessed the effects of the framing manipulation on the percentage of attributions citing either presidential responsibility, the release of the hostages, or specific foreign policy considerations (see figure 6.4).

Presidential responsibility peaked, as expected, in the Political Framing condition. Forty-one percent of all attributions referred to the personal traits of the president, a figure that was significantly higher than the comparable percentage in the Middle East condition. Presidential attributions were evenly divided between those referring to incompetence and untrustworthiness.

The degree to which the arms sale was attributed to specific foreign policy objectives also differed significantly across the three conditions. The Arms for Hostages condition elicited not one reference to specific policy considerations (other than the release of the hostages) and therefore diverged significantly from the remaining conditions. Citation of specific foreign policy goals (such as ending the Gulf War and improving relations with Iran) was most noticeable in the Middle East condition (44 percent of all responses). References to gaining the release of the hostages, however, were most frequent (outnumbering others by a ratio of two to one) when the news depicted the arms sale in this vein.

News reports that covered the arms deal from the perspective of Middle Eastern conflicts were clearly the most approval-enhancing; here reasoning about the policy considerations that could have led to the arms sale overshadowed references to the president's character or leadership by a margin of four to one. Conversely, political framing of the Iran-Contra affair proved most approval-diminishing; presidential responsibility for the decision was so amplified as to account for more than 40 percent of all the explanations in this condition.

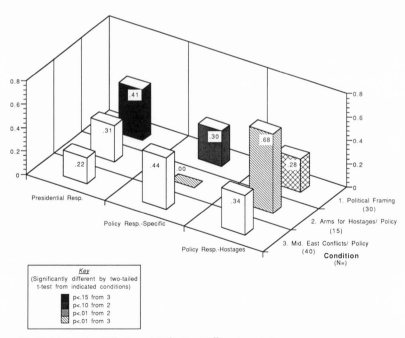

Fig. 6.4 Framing Effects on Attribution: Selling Arms to Iran

Conclusion

The results from the framing experiment indicate that Americans' attributions for the Iran arms sale were significantly molded by television news coverage. More often than not (66 percent of all stories), the networks covered the escalating political conflict and opposition to the president generated by the arms sale; this type of coverage clearly encouraged viewers to hold President Reagan personally responsible. In contrast, news coverage that focused on the ostensible policy objectives behind the arms sale led the viewing audience to consider situational antecedents of the decision by which the arms sale became a governmental response to foreign policy problems.

These results have important implications for attribution theory. Unlike the behavior of individual "actors" decisions taken by governments do not automatically elicit a preponderance of attributions rooted in political leaders' personal traits. Even when news reports discussed the Iran arms-sale decision explicitly as a case of inept leadership, viewers were not given to assign responsibility exclusively to the president. In general, policy goals tended to outweigh personal qualities as causal factors. What is particularly revealing is that even viewers who received no information about the particular role of the president and the political controversy over the president's leadership understood the Iran-Contra affair mainly in terms of institutional rather than personal responsibility.

More generally, these results mean that when individuals are called upon to explain a significant political decision rather than some trivial episode of everyday social behavior (which is the typical target of attribution experiments in social psychology), their attributions of responsibility are sophisticated rather than naive; instead of exaggerating the impact of the president and focusing exclusively on his personal traits, citizens give due consideration to institutional and contextual factors beyond the president's control.

Finally, the results suggest that network news can significantly affect presidential popularity. Previous analyses of popularity have shown that presidential rhetoric and other "image-building" efforts are generally ineffective in boosting popularity. Ostrom and Simon, for instance, found that the frequency of President Reagan's speeches had very modest effects on his popularity and that such forms of "political drama" failed to staunch the drop in his popularity during the Iran-Contra affair.[8] Although President Reagan's own efforts to avoid taking responsibility for the Iran-Contra affair may have been for nought, the evidence from the framing study indicates that patterns of news coverage did affect attributions of responsibility. The dominant political frame induced viewers to hold the president responsible; however, when the arms sale was described as an instrument of American foreign policy, viewers were much less likely to consider the president responsible. As chapter 8 will demonstrate, by affecting attributions of responsibility, network framing of the Iran-Contra affair also influenced evaluations of President Reagan.

SEVEN

Effects of Attributions on Issue-Specific Opinions

Attributions of causal and treatment responsibility are of interest only to the extent that they influence public opinion. This chapter uses correlational analysis to examine the relationship between attributions of responsibility and political opinions and concludes that attributions serve as important psychological cues for opinion formation.

The political opinions examined here fall into three categories. Evaluations of governmental performance consist of ratings of the performance of public officials (including the president) and institutions with respect to a "target" issue. Policy preferences relate to approval or disapproval of government-spending patterns and support of or opposition to specific policies or programs within issue areas. Finally, affect for various groups and individuals involved in each of the issue domains was also treated as an opinion.

As mentioned in chapter 1, there are substantial grounds for anticipating spillover effects from attributions of responsibility to political opinions. Attributions powerfully affect beliefs, attitudes, and even behaviors in a wide range of areas.[1] To assess the importance of attributions as opinion cues, composite or "net" indices of responsibility were computed for each participant. For the social welfare issues, the indices were computed by subtracting the percentage of individualistic attributions from the percentage of societal attributions.[2] For crime and terrorism, the summed percentages of individualistic and punitive attributions were subtracted from the percentage of societal attributions. The index for the Iran-Contra affair was computed by subtracting the percentage of policy attributions from the percentage of presidential attributions. Thus, higher scores on the responsibility index for poverty and racial inequality and unemployment indicated greater frequency of societal attributions. For crime and terrorism, higher scores on the responsibility index also measured greater frequency of societal (over punitive and individualistic) attributions. Finally, in the case of the Iran-Contra affair, higher scores on the index represented a higher occurrence of presidential attributions.

The results in chapters 4–6 have demonstrated that attributions of responsibility for political issues are significantly influenced by framing. The ability of news frames to alter attributions indicates that attributions can be thought of as short-lived factors that coexist in individuals' minds with a host of other important psychological cues, some of which have been internalized over the course of a lifetime. Political party identification and liberal-conservative orientation are perhaps the most relevant of such long-term, dispositional influences on public opinion,[3] and in all the correlational analyses described here, partisan and ideological differences were taken into account (see appendix C).

Social welfare issues are particularly apt to evoke partisan cleavages, and opinions concerning these issues were expected to reflect party identification. It was expected that Democrats would show greater support for social welfare and civil rights programs and express higher affect for groups or individuals who advocate or benefit from these programs than would Republicans. It was less clear how Democrats and Republicans would differ in their opinions toward crime and terrorism since neither political party has staked out a distinctive posture for these issues. Liberal versus conservative ideological orientation was also expected to evoke effects parallel to the Democratic versus Republican distinction. Evaluations of President Reagan, a strong conservative, were expected to be especially influenced by ideological bent.

In addition to partisanship and ideological orientation, factual knowledge may also influence political opinions. The analyses that follow incorporated a measure of information about each target issue (see appendix C). By controlling for the effects of information, the possibility that the observed effects of attributions on opinions were merely disguised effects of political information (i.e., more informed respondents might tend to say more in response to the questions on responsibility) was eliminated. Finally, the analyses also controlled for respondents' education and race.[4]

A final methodological point concerns the possibility that causal and treatment attributions influence issue opinions interactively. For example, respondents who attribute both causal and treatment responsibility for poverty to societal factors may be more likely to support social welfare programs than respondents who cite societal factors for only one form of responsibility. Preliminary analyses revealed several instances of such joint effects. Where appropriate, therefore, the analyses included a predictor variable representing the joint influence of causal and treatment attributions.[5]

Correlational analysis of the relationship between attributions and opinions can provide only an indirect test of the theoretical argument that television news influences attributions of responsibility, which, in turn, influence political opinions. While the working hypothesis underlying these analyses was that attributions are causes of opinions, it is, of course, possible that the causal direction is reversed and political opinions affect attributions. Individuals who like President Reagan, for instance, may deny that his cuts in social welfare benefits were responsible for causing poverty. To the extent possible, therefore, the correlational analyses employed here estimate the relative influence of attributions on opinions after "adjusting" for the influence of alternative antecedent factors such as party identification or information. Unfortunately, with the exception of the Iran-Contra affair (where the strong influence of party identification on attributions made this confusion over causal primacy most apparent), it was not possible to estimate systematically the extent of feedback from participants' political opinions to their attributions. In general, therefore, the results from the correlational analyses should be treated with caution.

To bolster confidence in the assumption that attribution is exogenous (i.e., that attributions are causal factors), three simple tests were carried out, and the results of each supported the assumption. First, with the exception of the Iran-Contra affair, attributions of responsibility were relatively uninfluenced by the most important antecedents of political opinions. Party affiliation and liberal-conservative orientation together explained, on average, less than 10 percent of the variation in attributions of causal and treatment responsibility for the target issues. Second, the independent effect of any particular opinion on other opinions was much weaker and less widespread than the independent effects of causal and treatment attributions. For instance, evaluations of President Reagan's performance concerning poverty exerted weaker influence on social welfare policy preferences than attributions of responsibility for poverty. Finally, and compellingly, a small number of significant differences between the experimental conditions emerged in the opinions under examination. For example, support for increased social welfare spending was lowered significantly under conditions of episodic framing of poverty.

The results of the correlational analyses are presented issue by issue. In the cases of poverty and the Iran-Contra affair, the results from the Suffolk County studies were replicated using national surveys.

Poverty

One of the experiments on poverty included a lengthy battery of questions probing opinions on a variety of poverty-related matters. Respondents evaluated how well President Reagan had coped with poverty and the federal budget deficit and rated the efforts of corporate leaders in reducing poverty. Individuals also indicated their preferences concerning the level of government spending on social welfare and defense (see appendix C). Multivariate analysis revealed the independent effects of attributions of causal and treatment responsibility, party affiliation, political ideology, and political information on opinions relating to poverty (see appendix C and table 7.1).

Attributions of causal responsibility for poverty proved to be powerful opinion cues in several instances, including evaluations of President Reagan's and business leaders' performance and preferences concerning levels of government spending for social welfare and defense. When causal responsibility was attributed to societal factors, evaluations of President Reagan and business leaders were much more negative, support for defense spending was lowered, and support for spending on social welfare was increased. In fact, the index of causal responsibility was the only antecedent factor that exerted significant effects on all five target opinions for poverty.

Attributions of treatment responsibility proved less influential as opinion cues, displaying only marginally significant effects on three of the five target opinions. Societal treatment attributions were associated with more critical evaluations of the president's performance, greater opposition to defense spending, and greater support for social welfare spending.

Among the control variables, partisanship and liberal-conservative

Table 7.1 Attribution of Responsibility as an Issue-Specific Opinion Cue: Poverty Experiment 2

	President's Performance		Business Leaders' Performance	Government-Spending Preferences	
	Budget	Poverty		Defense	Social Welfare
Index of causal re-	−.25****	−.41****	−.18***	−.51****	.41****
sponsibility	(.10)	(.07)	(.14)	(.14)	(.15)
Index of treatment	−.17**			−.24**	.26**
responsibility	(.10)			(.13)	(.14)
Democrats					.35*
					(.24)
Republicans	.55****	.65****	.27***	.45**	
	(.16)	(.14)	(.13)	(26)	
Liberals	−.49****			−.51***	
	(.17)			(.27)	
Conservatives		.32***		.66***	
		(.16)		(.31)	
Information			.12***		
			(.06)		
N	223	226	220	225	234

Notes: Table entries are unstandardized regression coefficients (ols) with standard errors given in parentheses. Blank entries indicate nonsignificant coefficients.
****$p < .01$; ***$p < .05$; **$p < .10$; *$p < .15$.

orientation both provided a strong impetus for poverty opinions. Republicans and conservatives rated the president's performance with respect to poverty positively, while liberals (though not Democrats) rated his performance negatively. A similar division prevailed for defense-spending preferences. On the other hand, factual knowledge proved irrelevant as a cue for opinions concerning poverty.

Data from the 1985 National Pilot Survey carried out by the Center for Political Studies were used to replicate the results reported above. Specifically, this survey included a battery of closed-ended rating items designed to assess causal attributions of poverty. These items fell into two categories of attributions—societal and individualistic—and therefore matched the open-ended responses to the "most important causes" question used in the Suffolk County studies. Additive indices of societal and individualistic causal responsibility were computed and then subtracted from each other; the higher the difference score, the more importance respondents attached to societal (over individualistic) causes (see appendix C). In addition, the Pilot Survey also included items measuring respondents' beliefs about the efficacy of individual effort and work as determinants of economic mobility. Three such items were used to construct a surrogate index of societal treatment attributions. High scorers were those who believed that individuals do not control their economic destiny (see appendix C).

The Pilot Survey also provided measures of factual information from which those most germane to poverty were selected to construct an additive index of factual information. The standard party identification and liberal-conservative questions were used to construct dichotomous variables corresponding to Democrats, Republicans, liberals, and conservatives. Finally, to replicate the earlier analyses fully, respondents' education and race were also taken into account when predicting their opinions.

The criterion opinions themselves were selected so as to match those used in the Suffolk County experiments. They included assessments of President Reagan's performance, social welfare policy preferences, and affect for the poor. (See table 7.2.)

There were eight criterion opinions in this analysis. The index of causal responsibility exerted significant effects on seven of the eight. Individuals making more societal attributions felt more warmly toward poor people, blacks, and those on welfare. They also evaluated President Reagan's economic performance negatively and favored increased government spending for social welfare, government jobs, and minority-assistance programs. The index of treatment responsibility affected evaluations of presidential performance, social welfare spending, and affect for the poor—the higher the level of societal treatment attributions, the more critical the evaluation of presidential performance, the greater the support for minority-assistance programs, and the higher the level of affect for poor people.

In addition to attributions of responsibility, party identification and liberal-conservative orientation both proved influential, especially with regard to assessments of presidential performance and support for social welfare spending. The indicators of affect for poor people and blacks, however, were *entirely unaffected* by partisan and ideological considerations; here, the *only* relevant cues were attributions.

All in all, the national survey results parallel the Suffolk County results quite closely. Americans who held society responsible for pov-

Table 7.2 Attribution of Responsibility as an Issue-Specific Opinion Cue: 1985 NES Pilot Survey

	President's Performance		Government-Spending Preferences				Affect		
	Budget	Economy	Welfare	Jobs	Help Minorities	Poor People	Poor People	Blacks	Welfare Recipients
Index of causal responsibility		−.05*** (.02)	.10*** (.02)	.04** (.02)	.07*** (.02)	.40* (.22)		1.04*** (.21)	.61** (.26)
Index of treatment responsibility	−.12*** (.03)	−.09*** (.05)			.07** (.03)	.75** (.35)			
Democrats	−.87*** (.19)	−.73*** (.17)	.57** (.20)						7.60*** (2.40)
Republicans	.76*** (.22)	.63*** (.20)		−.40** (.19)					
Liberals			.79*** (.36)	.63** (.31)	.65** (.31)				8.11** (4.12)
Conservatives	.41* (.24)	.50** (.22)	.50* (.27)						
Information	−.27*** (.07)		−.34** (.08)	−.16** (.07)					−2.43*** (.87)
N	290	308	305	286	290	305		307	308

Notes: Table entries are unstandardized regression coefficients (ols) with standard errors given in parentheses. Blank entries indicate nonsignificant coefficients.

***$p < .01$; **$p < .05$; *$p < .10$.

erty were more critical of President Reagan's performance concerning the issue, were more supportive of "activist" social welfare policies, and were more empathic toward the beneficiaries of these policies. Although the effects of attributions did not overwhelm the effects of alternative antecedents to the same degree as in the Suffolk County experiments, there can be no doubt that attributions of responsibility independently and powerfully dictated the shape of public opinion toward poverty.

Racial Inequality

In the area of race, the target opinions included President Reagan's performance on civil rights; federal government spending for "assistance to blacks"; government programs to "help improve the social and economic position of blacks and other racial minorities"; and affect for civil rights leaders, Jesse Jackson, and black people in general. (See appendix C and table 7.3.)

In contrast to poverty, where causal attributions were the dominant cue, treatment and causal attributions both extended powerful effects on racial attitudes. Individuals who held society responsible for treating racial inequality were more supportive of government efforts to help minorities and increased federal spending on civil rights programs. They also expressed greater affect for black people, civil rights leaders in general, and Jesse Jackson in particular. President Reagan's performance on civil rights was the only target opinion untouched by treatment attributions.

While somewhat overshadowed by treatment attributions, the effects of causal attributions on racial opinions were robust in five of the six instances. Societal causal attributions induced greater support for civil rights programs and federal spending to assist minorities. Respondents who cited societal causes also expressed higher affect for civil rights leaders and black people. In addition, societal causal attributions weakened approval of President Reagan's performance.

Among the other potential cues, liberal-conservative orientation was frequently influential; liberals felt more warmly toward civil rights leaders and Jesse Jackson and assessed President Reagan's record on civil rights more harshly, while conservatives were cool toward civil rights leaders and assessed President Reagan's civil rights record more positively. With only one exception (Republicans evaluated Reagan's record on civil rights more negatively), partisan

Table 7.3 Attribution of Responsibility as an Issue-Specific Opinion Cue: Racial Inequality

	President's Performance	Government-Spending Preferences		Affect		
		Help Minorities	Civil Rights	Civil Rights Leaders	Jesse Jackson	Black People
Index of causal responsibility	−.24***	.70****	.27****	3.95*		3.16*
	(.10)	(.18)	(.06)	(2.46)		(2.21)
Index of treatment responsibility		.29**	.25***	6.11***	5.36***	6.59****
		(.17)	(.06)	(2.33)	(2.37)	(2.11)
Democrats						
Republicans	.51****					
	(.17)					
Liberals	−.43****			10.18***	13.20***	
	(.19)			(4.91)	(5.80)	
Conservatives	.32**			−15.51****		
	(.20)			(4.95)		
Information	−.14****				3.53****	2.21***
	(.05)				(1.32)	(1.20)
N	247	246	231	255	260	256

Notes: Table entries are unstandardized regression coefficients (ols) with standard errors given in parentheses. Blank entries indicate nonsignificant coefficients.

****$p < .01$; ***$p < .05$; **$p < .10$; *$p < .15$.

differences in racial attitudes were conspicuously absent. Finally, factual information also influenced racial opinions; the more informed respondents were more critical of President Reagan's record and responded more positively toward blacks and Jesse Jackson.

Overall, attributions of responsibility were strong cues for racial opinions. The effects of treatment attributions consistently outstripped the effects of partisanship, liberal-conservative orientation, and factual information. Although secondary to questions of treatment, causal attributions also structured opinions on racial issues.

Crime

In the area of crime, the criterion opinions included support for the death penalty, evaluations of presidential performance and the performance of judges, preferences concerning government spending on "law enforcement," and affect for the police (See appendix C and table 7.4.)

Table 7.4 Attribution of Responsibility as an Issue-Specific Opinion Cue: Crime

	Death Penalty	Affect: Police	Judges' Performance	President's Performance	Law Enforcement Spending
Index of causal responsibility	$-.35$****	-3.58***	$-.13$**	$-.12$***	$.07$**
	(.15)	(1.77)	(.07)	(.08)	(.04)
Index of treatment responsibility	-1.26****	-7.50****		$-.28$****	$-.25$****
	(.21)	(2.39)		(.08)	(.04)
Causal × treatment responsibility	$-.49$****	-4.69***		$-.16$***	
	(.19)	(2.22)		(.08)	
Democrats					
Republicans		6.37*	.32**	.57****	
		(4.17)	(.17)	(.15)	
Liberals					
Conservatives			.43***	.38***	
			(.21)	(.19)	
Information		4.67**			
		(2.58)			
N	249	260	235	231	254

Notes: Entries are unstandardized regression coefficients (ols) with standard errors given in parentheses. Blank entries indicate nonsignificant coefficients.
****$p < .01$; ***$p < .05$; **$p < .10$; *$p < .15$.

For crime, more than any other issue, attributions of responsibility completely overshadowed partisanship, liberal-conservative orientation, and information in influencing opinions and attitudes. Societal attributions for crime—both causal and treatment—entailed opposition to the death penalty and a relatively scathing assessment of President Reagan's performance. Those who offered more societal attributions also evaluated judges more critically and expressed less support for the police, although the former effect was limited to causal attributions. Finally, the effects of causal and treatment attributions diverged with respect to government spending on "law enforcement." Societal causal attributions increased support (albeit marginally) for increased spending, while societal treatment attributions exerted an effect in the opposite direction. This inconsistency may stem from the ambiguity of the attitude stimulus. Some respondents may have interpreted federal spending on "law enforcement" to refer to strengthened punitive measures or agents (such as more police), while others may have interpreted the term more broadly (for example, more funds for prisoner rehabilitation programs).

Not only did attributions of causal and treatment responsibility independently influence opinions, but there were three significant joint, or interaction, effects. The interaction effects were traced to the pairing of societal causal attributions with punitive treatment attributions, which instilled particularly extreme opinions. This particular combination of causal and treatment responsibility was characterized by the highest level of support for President Reagan's performance concerning crime, the highest level of affect for the police, and the greatest enthusiasm for the death penalty. Under this combination, agents or programs of social control were evaluated favorably since they were absolved of causal responsibility yet granted a significant degree of treatment responsibility for crime. When causal and treatment responsibility were both attributed to the absence of firm punitive measures, however, law enforcement agents or processes represented causes of crime as well as treatment. Evaluations of these targets were therefore moderated accordingly.

The results of the analysis are remarkable not only for the significant influence of attributions, but also for the degree to which crime-related opinions were immune to the effects of long-standing dispositional characteristics—partisanship, liberal-conservative placement, and knowledge. Only six significant effects were exerted by these dispositional antecedents compared with a total of twelve exerted by attributions. Since crime is an issue of considerable personal relevance, the weakness of partisan or ideological differences is strong testimony to the psychological power of attributions.

Terrorism

The second terrorism experiment included several criterion opinions, including evaluations of President Reagan's and the Israeli government's performance in dealing with terrorism, affect for Libya's Colonel Qaddafi and the U.S. military, preferences concerning government spending on "antiterrorist measures" and support for the "use of U.S. military force against governments that aid terrorists." (See appendix C and table 7.5.)

Treatment attributions permeated opinions about terrorism. Individuals who cited societal treatment attributions were more critical of President Reagan and the government of Israel, expressed less affect for the military, opposed the use of military force against governments that assist terrorists, opposed increased federal spending on antiterrorist measures, and were less antagonistic toward Colonel Qaddafi.[6] In short, the question of whether societal reform or greater punitive measures are the appropriate means of treating international terrorism was fundamental to individuals' opinions.

The effects of causal attributions were limited to only two of the six criterion opinions. Those who offered more societal causal attributions were more opposed to the use of military force against governments aiding terrorists and were less supportive of government spending for antiterrorist measures. In the case of terrorism, treatment attributions took precedence over causal attributions as opinion cues.

Significant interaction effects emerged for three of the six opinions. As was the case with the results for crime, the source of these joint effects was the combination of societal causal attributions (for example, discrimination as a cause of terrorism) and punitive treatment attributions. Under this particular mix of causal and treatment responsibility, respondents expressed the most support for President Reagan's performance, government spending on antiterrorist programs, and the military. Once again, this particular combination of attributions generated the highest level of support for agents or programs of social control because such agents were absolved of causal responsibility yet granted a significant degree of treatment responsi-

Table 7.5 Attribution of Responsibility as an Issue-Specific Opinion Cue: Terrorism Experiment 2

	Performance		Policy Preferences		Affect	
	President	Israelis	Use of Force	Antiterrorism Spending	Quaddafi	U.S. Military
Index of causal responsibility			-.33***	-.19****		-11.21***
			(.17)	(.05)		(2.42)
Index of treatment responsibility	-.49****	-.26****	-.82****	-.19****	3.40***	-3.95*
	(.10)	(.10)	(.17)	(.06)	(1.35)	(2.77)
Causal × treatment responsibility	-.18**			-.14****		-7.18*
	(.11)			(.06)		(4.33)
Democrats		-.33**	-1.13****	-.21***		14.43****
		(.18)	(.32)	(.10)		(4.88)
Republicans		.36**	.79***			
		(.20)	(.36)			
Liberals						
Conservatives	.42**		.70**	.21**		
	(.24)		(.42)	(.12)		
Information			.40****			
			(.14)			
N	254	219	251	239	211	255

Notes: Table entries are unstandardized regression coefficients (ols) with standard errors given in parentheses. Blank entries indicate nonsignificant coefficients.
****$p < .01$; ***$p < .05$; **$p < .10$; *$p < .15$.

bility. By contrast, from the perspective of those individuals who assigned both causal and treatment responsibility to inadequate punitive measures, the actions of President Reagan and the U.S. military represent *both* causes (the government fails to mete out stiff retribution, hence terrorism) and treatments. Under the combination of punitive causal and treatment attributions, therefore, individuals were more ambivalent in their attitudes toward public officials or institutions.

As expected, liberal-conservative orientation was less relevant to opinions concerning terrorism than to opinions concerning poverty or racial inequality. Contrary to expectations, partisanship was a potent cue; Republicans evaluated the military and Israel more favorably and were more inclined to favor military retaliation, while Democrats were more opposed to the use of military force, favored less spending on antiterrorist measures, and evaluated Israel and the military more unfavorably.

Foreign Policy Opinions

The Iran-Contra Experiment

The Iran-Contra study included a lengthy battery of questions concerning matters of foreign policy and terrorism, including evaluations of President Reagan's performance in the areas of "foreign policy," "terrorism," and "reducing tensions with the Soviet Union." Respondents also indicated their preferences concerning government spending on "antiterrorist measures." Finally, they expressed either support for or opposition to military (as opposed to diplomatic) sanctions against governments known to assist terrorists, greater U.S. involvement in Central America, and increased cooperation with the Soviet Union. (See appendix C and table 7.6.)

All three performance ratings were significantly affected by Iran-Contra attributions; individuals who considered the president responsible were much less approving of his performance than individuals who cited policy explanations for the arms sale. Surprisingly, this effect was strongest for ratings of the president's performance in "reducing tensions" with the Soviets, the performance area most distant from the Iran-Contra decision.

The relevance of attributions to foreign policy preferences was less clear-cut. Unlike assessments of President Reagan's performance,

Table 7.6 Attribution of Responsibility as a Foreign Policy Opinion Cue: The Iran-Contra Study

	President's Performance				Policy Preferences		
	Foreign Policy	Global Tensions	Terrorism	Antiterrorism Spending	Use of Force	US/USSR Relations	Cent. Amer.
Index of presidential responsibility	-.26***	-.63****	-.36****	-.25****		.56***	
	(.12)	(.14)	(.14)	(.08)		(.25)	
Democrats	-.72****			-.36***			
	(.25)			(.19)			
Republicans	.41**	.46**	.63***				-.90*
	(.24)	(.25)	(.28)				(.61)
Liberals					-1.53**		1.38**
					(.86)		(.81)
Conservatives					1.01*	-1.42***	
					(.74)	(.65)	
Information							
N	76	79	73	70	74	73	57

Notes: Table entries are unstandardized regression coefficients (ols) with standard errors given in parentheses. Blank entries indicate nonsignificant coefficients. The measure of attribution is the percentage of responses citing presidential responsibility minus the percentage citing policy factors.

****$p < .01$; ***$p < .05$; **$p < .10$; *$p < .15$.

where attributions and party affiliation were the major influences, the policy preferences were governed primarily by partisan and ideological orientation. Individuals who held the president responsible for the arms sale were opposed to greater spending on antiterrorism measures and also favored greater cooperation with the Soviets, but attributions made no difference to support for or opposition to intervention in Central America or military retaliation against governments that aided terrorists.

"CBS News"–New York Times Surveys

The surveys conducted by "CBS News" and the *New York Times* in the aftermath of the Iran-Contra disclosures permit an unusually detailed replication of the results noted above. The 16 July 1987 survey is particularly valuable for its inclusion of an open-ended question concerning the issues on which respondents felt Colonel North had not testified truthfully. Respondents who indicated that Colonel North had concealed the degree of President Reagan's involvement were treated as "presidential attributors" who were compared with all others (including respondents who did not answer the question). Not surprisingly, this simple dichotomy was strongly correlated with responses to the standard "did the president know" question. The two questions were therefore combined to form an index of presidential responsibility. High scorers were individuals who imputed responsibility to the president (see appendix C).

The criterion opinions were drawn from two levels—Iran-Contra–related opinions and opinions on foreign policy matters that did not directly bear on Iran-Contra events. The former set included evaluations of "how well President Reagan is handling the whole issue of arms sales and the Contras," support for Contra military aid, approval of Colonel North, the perceived significance of "the Iran-Contra matter" for the country, and, finally, assessments of the harshness or leniency (toward the president) of the Tower Commission Report (see appendix C).

The second level of analysis assessed the degree to which attribution of presidential responsibility for the arms sale penetrated a layer of foreign policy opinions not directly related to Iran-Contra events or issues. This set of opinions included evaluations of the president's handling of foreign policy in general, his handling of arms control negotiations with the Soviet Union, respondents' relative confidence in

Congress versus President Reagan "to make the right decisions on foreign policy," approval of Secretary of State George Schultz, support for the second Strategic Arms Limitation Talks (SALT 2), and, finally, opinions concerning whether President Reagan had restored international respect for the United States (see appendix C).

To assess the effects of attributions of responsibility for the arms sale on foreign policy opinions, the indicator of presidential responsibility was first purged of partisan and ideological influence. This procedure has the beneficial effect of reducing the scope of "rationalization bias" in attributions. As documented in chapter 6, Republicans and conservatives differed systematically from Democrats and liberals in their willingness to hold the president responsible. By first adjusting the indicator of presidential responsibility for such defensive attribution mechanisms, a relatively "clean" estimate of the degree to which foreign policy opinions were affected by attributions for the arms sale was obtained. Finally, to parallel the earlier analyses, respondents' political information, education, and race were also taken into account when predicting their foreign policy opinions. (See appendix C and table 7.7.)

In all five tests, attributions independently influenced opinions. Individuals assigning responsibility to the president felt the Iran-Contra issue was a more significant national problem, opposed military aid for the Contras, disapproved of Colonel North, judged the Tower Commission Report to have been too lenient, and rated President Reagan's performance more severely. In three of the five issue-specific tests (Iran-Contra salience, arms sale performance, Tower Commission Report), the effects of presidential attributions outstripped the effects of political party affiliation. Considering the stringent specification employed in these analyses (namely, the purging of partisan and ideological influence from the measure of attribution), the results of the analysis are particularly compelling: attribution of responsibility for the arms sale proved to be a highly relevant cue for Iran-Contra opinions.

Attributions also colored foreign policy opinions not immediately linked to the Iran-Contra matter (table 7.8). Attributions of responsibility exerted a significant effect on all seven such opinions. Individuals holding President Reagan responsible preferred to never negotiate with terrorists and evaluated the president's performance on arms control and foreign policy negatively. They also opposed the

Table 7.7 Attribution of Responsibility for the Arms Sale and Iran-Contra Opinions: "CBS News"–*New York Times* Surveys

	Contra Aid[a]	Issue Salience[a]	Tower Report[b]	Col. North[a]	Reagan's Performance
Index of presidential responsibility	−.40**** (.08)	.16**** (.03)	.15**** (.02)	−.21**** (.08)	−.23**** (.03)
Democrats		.12*** (.05)			−.13**** (.03)
Republicans	.40**** (.12)	−.08** (.05)	−.26**** (.04)	.40**** (.13)	.20**** (.04)
Liberals			†		
Conservatives		−.09** (.05)	†		.06*** (.03)
Information	.26**** (.07)	−.05* (.03)		.12** (.07)	.03* (.02)
N	551	590	942	664	820

Notes: Table entries are unstandardized regression coefficients (ols) with standard errors given in parentheses. Blank entries indicate nonsignificant coefficients.
[a]16 July 1987 survey.
[b]28 February 1987 survey.
[c]7–8 December 1986 survey.
†Items not included in survey.
****$p < .01$; ***$p < .05$; **$p < .10$; *$p < .15$.

administration's efforts to bypass the SALT 2 agreement (although here the majority of respondents had no opinion) and were more critical of the secretary of state. Finally, individuals attributing responsibility to the president opposed granting the president the right to conduct covert operations overseas and felt that President Reagan had not raised the stock of the United States abroad. The effects of attributions were not as powerful as the effects of party affiliation, but they easily surpassed the effects of political ideology and information.

Conclusion

Network framing has important consequences for public opinion. For crime and terrorism, the dominant episodic news frame, by strengthening attributions of punitive and individualistic responsibility,

Table 7.8 Attribution of Responsibility for the Arms Sale and Foreign Policy Opinions: "CBS News"–*New York Times* Surveys

	Policy Preferences				President's Performance		
	Negotiated[d] with terrorists	SALT 2[c] Agreement	Sec.[b] of State	Covert[a] Operations	Respect[c] for U.S.	Foreign[a] Policy	Arms[b] Control
Index of presidential responsibility	−.06**** (.02)	.12**** (.04)	−.10**** (.03)	−.16**** (.03)	−.28**** (.03)	−.28**** (.03)	−.13**** (.02)
Democrats		.17*** (.06)	−.10* (.06)	−.11*** (.05)	−.14**** (.04)	−.22**** (.04)	−.17**** (.04)
Republicans	.15**** (.05)	−.24**** (.07)	.19**** (.06)	.13*** (.05)	.18**** (.04)	.16**** (.05)	.16**** (.05)
Liberals	†	†	†	−.08* (.05)		−.16**** (.05)	†
Conservatives	†	†	†		.12**** (.04)	.10*** (.04)	†
Information		−.09*** (.04)		.04** (.02)		.05*** (.02)	
N	551	319	743	631	913	582	973

Notes: Table entries are unstandardized regression coefficients (ols) with standard errors given in parentheses. Blank entries indicate nonsignificant coefficients.

[a]16 July 1987 survey.

[b]28 February 1987 survey.

[c]7–8 December 1986 survey.

[d]30 November 1986 survey.

†Item not included in survey.

****$p < .01$; ***$p < .05$; **$p < .10$; *$p < .15$.

indirectly increased support for measures such as the death penalty and military reprisals against "terrorist" states. Episodic framing of poverty indirectly reduced public support for social welfare programs and increased public approval of leaders committed to slashing such programs. These results suggest that the widely heralded shifts in American public opinion during the 1980s toward a "law and order" stance on issues of public security and "less government" in areas of social welfare have occurred not only because of the repeated election of conservative presidents or because of gradual shifts in the public's partisan and ideological affinities, but also because of patterns of television news coverage in which poverty, crime, and terrorism are depicted overwhelmingly as concrete episodes.

In the case of the Iran-Contra affair, the results indicate that television news proved damaging to the Reagan administration. By suggesting that the president was responsible for the arms sale, the dominant political frame indirectly eroded public support for the president and his subordinates. Similarly, Americans who held the president responsible were much less supportive of key elements of the administration's foreign policy, including covert operations and Contra aid.

The power of attributions over opinions concerning specific issues may be driven by the rule of simplicity. Citizens follow an elementary rule: oppose policies, institutions, groups, or leaders who represent forces of problem causation and support institutions, programs, or leaders who represent forces of treatment. In this sense, attributions of responsibility are potent "heuristics" for overcoming the complexity of public issues.

While the results reported in this chapter suggest a close connection between attribution and opinion, it must be admitted that to this point the contest between attributions and alternative dispositional antecedents of political opinions, such as party identification or ideological preference, has been inherently unfair. Attributions of responsibility are issue-specific cues, while partisanship and ideology are global cues. Individuals must perform more inferential work to get from their ideology or party preference to opinions concerning specific issues; thus, it is not surprising that attributions seem more powerful in affecting issue-specific opinions than the dispositional cues.

Just as the leap from ideology or party identification to issue-specific opinions is longer than the leap from attributions to issue-specific opinions, the leap from attributions to general opinions should be longer than the leap from party identification or ideology. A more stringent comparison of the relative influence of attributions and dispositional cues is to examine their effects on general opinions. The next chapter turns to this question.

EIGHT

Effects of Attributions on General Opinions

This chapter considers the extent to which attributions of responsibility for political issues color individuals' general opinions of their leaders, especially the president. Since attributions will influence general opinions only to the extent that individuals extend their reasoning about the causes and treatments of particular issues beyond the immediate subject matter of these issues, the demonstration of such influence provides a much stronger statement about the political significance of network framing effects than the results presented in the preceding chapter.

Three different general political evaluations concerning the president (in all cases Reagan) will be addressed: his overall performance in office, his competence, and his integrity. The president's overall performance is the typical barometer of his popularity, while competence and integrity are both bellwether traits in the public image of the president.[1] For each of these evaluations of the president, two separate analyses were carried out corresponding to the "direct" and "indirect" effects of attributions of responsibility.

It is assumed that evaluations of the president may be directly influenced by attributions. The attribution of poverty to societal forces, for instance, may be a direct cause of disapproval of the president simply because he is a highly visible political force. It is further assumed that evaluations of the president may be indirectly affected by attributions because, depending upon the direction of the attribution (e.g., societal or individualistic), issue-specific opinions become more or less prominent in the formation of general opinions. The indirect effects hypothesis assumes specifically that when citizens make societal attributions for issues they become "politicized," that is, they tend to focus on their issue-specific opinions when forming their general impressions of political leaders. In other words, societal attributions "energize" issue-specific opinions as criteria for evaluations of the president. In the case of poverty, for example, the assumption is that respondents who attribute responsibility to societal factors will evaluate the president more in terms of their social welfare policy preferences and his performance concerning poverty than will respondents who attribute responsibility to individuals. If it is the poor and not society who are held responsible for causing and curing poverty, then the efforts of the president to strengthen or curtail social welfare programs would seem to be of little consequence. In contrast, attributing responsibility to society implies that the president's actions are instrumental in affecting the level of poverty and, therefore, are more revealing of the effectiveness of his leadership or the strength of his character.[2]

Previous experimental studies have demonstrated that when television news coverage highlights attributions of societal responsibility for national issues (e.g., news reports that documented the effects of President Reagan's cuts in employment-training programs on unemployment), viewers' overall evaluations of the president become significantly more dependent upon their assessment of the president's performance concerning specific issues. Conversely, when news stories provided alternative (and nonsocietal) attributions of responsibility, the impact of viewers' ratings of the president's performance in specific issue areas on overall evaluations was weakened.[3] Generalizing from this evidence, the critical prediction is that societal attributions of responsibility will strengthen the connections between issue-specific and general opinions.

Three separate tests of direct and indirect effects were carried out. The first was limited to the issue of poverty and drews on evidence from the second framing experiment on poverty and from the 1985 NES Pilot Survey. The second test encompassed multiple issues and considered the relative importance of attributions for crime, terrorism, and racial inequality as cues for evaluating the president. The third test addressed the connections between attributions of responsibility for the Iran arms sale and general political evaluations and drews on evidence from both the framing experiment and the national surveys.

Direct Effects

Poverty

Among participants in the second framing experiment for poverty, causal (but not treatment) attributions were relevant cues for evaluating President Reagan. Societal attributions engendered more critical evaluations of President Reagan's overall performance, competence, and integrity. The effects of attributions, however, paled in comparison with the effects of party identification and political ideology (see appendix C and table 8.1).

Although attributions were measured differently in the NES Pilot Survey, the pattern of results was uniform with one exception; among NES respondents, causal and treatment attributions were *both* relevant standards for evaluating the president. Respondents who agreed with societal causal attributions for poverty were significantly more critical of President Reagan's competence and integrity, while those who favored societal intervention as the treatment for poverty were more critical of him on both trait ratings as well as overall performance. Once again, the effects of attributions were dwarfed by the effects of party identification and political ideology. Overall, both studies suggest that attributions of responsibility for poverty were only weak cues for general opinions.

Crime, Terrorism, and Racial Inequality

Crime was more connotative an issue than either terrorism or racial inequality. (See table 8.2.) Causal attributions for crime powerfully influenced all three general opinions, while treatment attributions influenced evaluations of overall presidential performance and presidential competence. In each case, the higher the frequency of societal attributions, the less positive the evaluation of President Reagan (see appendix C).

Attribution of treatment (but not causal) responsibility for terrorism also proved to be an important standard for evaluating the president. When treatment responsibility was assigned to society, approval of the president declined. Causal (but not treatment) attributions for racial inequality independently influenced all three evaluations of the president. The higher the frequency of societal attributions, the more negative the evaluation of President Reagan.

Table 8.1 Attribution of Responsibility and General Evaluations of the President: Poverty

	Performance		Competence		Integrity	
	Suffolk County	NES	Suffolk County	NES	Suffolk County	NES
Index of causal re-sponsibility	-.41****		-.33****	-.06***	-.49****	-.05**
	(.10)		(.12)	(.03)	(.14)	(.03)
Index of treatment responsibility		-.07****		-.10****		-.15****
		(.03)		(.04)		(.05)
Democrats		-.97****		-1.18****		-1.30****
		(.17)		(.25)		(.32)
Republicans	.70****	.53****	.70****	.62***	1.14****	1.12****
	(.16)	(.18)	(.21)	(.29)	(.25)	(.34)
Liberals	-.45****	-.63***	-1.00****	-1.16****	-.54***	-1.78****
	(.19)	(.28)	(.25)	(.39)	(.27)	(.50)
Conservatives	.44**	.38**	.42*	.65***	.68***	.75***
	(.20)	(.21)	(.26)	(.31)	(.28)	(.36)
Information						
N	238	300	215	307	198	296

Notes: Table entries are unstandardized regression coefficients (ols) with standard errors given in parentheses. Blank entries indicate nonsignificant coefficients.

**** $p < .01$; *** $p < .05$; ** $p < .10$; * $p < .15$.

Table 8.2 Attribution of Responsibility and General Evaluations of the President; Crime, Terrorism and Racial Inequality

	Performance	Competence	Integrity
Index of causal responsi-	−.24****	−.37****	−.38***
bility/crime	(.09)	(.14)	(.14)
Index of treatment re-	−.23****	−.17*	
sponsibility/crime	(.09)	(.12)	
Index of causal responsi-			
bility/terrorism			
Index of treatment re-	−.21***	−.27***	−.34****
sponsibility/terrorism	(.08)	(.12)	(.12)
Index of causal responsi-	−.23****	−.28***	−.24**
bility/inequality	(.09)	(.13)	(.14)
Index of treatment re-			
sponsibility/inequality			
Democrats	−.27**	−.54***	−.47***
	(.15)	(.22)	(.24)
Republicans	.40***	.51***	.48***
	(.17)	(.25)	(.24)
Liberals	−.42***		−.75***
	(.20)		(.32)
Conservatives	.37**		
	(.21)		
Information	−.03*	−.09****	
	(.02)	(.03)	
N	263	234	215

Notes: Table entries are unstandardized regression coefficients (ols) with standard errors given in parentheses. Blank entries indicate nonsignificant coefficients.
****$p < .01$; ***$p < .05$; **$p < .10$; *$p < .15$.

Among the control variables, partisanship was again the most compelling cue for general evaluations. Differences between Democrats and Republicans consistently exceeded differences between societal and individualistic attributors. Attributions, however, proved more influential than liberal-conservative orientation. Political information also discriminated between general opinions; the more informed were more critical of the president.

The Iran Arms Sale

Given the facts of the Iran arms sale (i.e., a covert action carried out by members of President Reagan's senior staff), attributions were expected to be particularly powerful cues; the higher the frequency of presidential attributions for the arms sale, the more negative the evaluations of the president. (See table 8.3.)

Attributions of presidential responsibility did predict general evaluations; individuals who considered the president responsible were more likely to downgrade his overall performance, competence, and integrity. These results suggest that the dominant political frame for the Iran sale (which dwelled on President Reagan's actions and the controversy they generated) inflicted considerable damage to the president's normally high popularity and likability, resulting in the lowest level of popularity of his second term.[4]

As usual, the impact of partisanship on President Reagan's standing was overwhelming. Ideological differences, however, were infrequent and political information proved irrelevant to general evaluations. In this particular test, therefore, attributions rivalled party identification as the principal antecedent of presidential evaluations.

The various "CBS News"–*New York Times* surveys conducted during the Iran-Contra affair permit a detailed replication of the above results. These surveys regularly included the popularity question in addition to questions bearing on President Reagan's leadership skills

Table 8.3 Attribution of Responsibility and General Evaluation of the President: The Iran Arms Sale

	Performance	Competence	Integrity
Index of presidential	−.38***	−.25**	−.42***
responsibility	(.12)	(.14)	(.17)
Democrats	−.68***		
	(.24)		
Republicans	.54***	.92***	1.25***
	(.24)	(.27)	(.36)
Liberals	−.66**		−.70*
	(.34)		(.40)
Conservatives			
Information			
N	85	85	85

Notes: Entries are unstandardized regression coefficients (ols) with standard errors given in parentheses. Blank entries indicate nonsignificant coefficients.
***$p < .01$; **$p < .05$; *$p < .10$.

and honesty. As an added bonus, one of the surveys also included a question probing evaluations of Vice President Bush as well as questions assessing trust in the federal government. Two separate analyses (based on the November 1986 and 16 July 1987 surveys) investigated the influence of attributions of presidential responsibility for the arms sale on general political evaluations (see appendix C and table 8.4).

In both surveys, evaluations of President Reagan's overall performance were significantly influenced by attributions of presidential responsibility for the arms sale.[5] President Reagan's image was noticeably harmed when citizens held him responsible. Although not as overriding an influence as party identification, attributions were more influential than either political ideology or political information. Attributing responsibility to the president also induced significant downward movement in approval of Vice President Bush and ratings of Reagan's competence and integrity. Finally, attributions for the arms sale significantly increased distrust of the federal government. In every instance, however, the influence of party identification exceeded the influence of attribution.

The results from the various correlational analyses suggest that attributions of responsibility are secondary to partisanship as a basis for forming general impressions of political leaders. Nevertheless, even after allowing for the effects of partisanship, ideology, and information, attributions did significantly influence how Americans evaluate their president. Presidential evaluations become less sanguine when individuals hold society responsible for national issues. By depicting issues through particular news frames, therefore, television indirectly affects how much popular support public officials can enjoy.

Indirect Effects

Indirect effects concern the degree to which the effects of issue-specific opinions on general opinions are strengthened when individuals make societal (but not individualistic) attributions. For each of the issue targets under analysis, three specific opinions were selected to test this prediction. Typically, these included the rating of presidential performance concerning the target, the question on government spending (in the case of the "CBS News"–*New York Times* survey the question on the importance of the Iran-Contra issue was substituted), and one additional policy preference. Methodological

Table 8.4 Attribution of Responsibility for the Iran-Contra Affair and General Evaluations of the President: "CBS News"–*New York Times* Surveys

	Presidential Evaluations						
	Performance		Competence		Integrity (11/86)	Eval. of Bush (11/86)	Trust in Government (11/86)
	(11/86)[a]	(7/87)[b]	(11/86)	(7/87)			
Index of presidential responsibility	−.15***	−.27***	−.66***	−.13***	−.16***	−.22***	−.28***
	(.02)	(.03)	(.08)	(.03)	(.02)	(.05)	(.04)
Democrats	−.25***	−.20***	−.62***	−.18***	−.12***	−.43***	−.25***
	(.04)	(.04)	(.14)	(.05)	(.04)	(.08)	(.09)
Republicans	.24***	.19***	.87***	.11***	.21***	.33***	.28**
	(.03)	(.04)	(.15)	(.05)	(.05)	(.06)	(.10)
Liberals	†	−.11**	†		†	†	†
		(.04)					
Conservatives	†	.09**	†		†	†	†
		(.04)					
Information	.04**	.04**					.11**
	(.02)	(.02)					(.04)
N	611	591	550	616	618	477	644

Notes: Table entries are unstandardized regression coefficients (ols) with standard errors given in parentheses. Blank entries indicate nonsignificant coefficients.

[a]7–8 December 1986 survey.
[b]16 July 1987 survey.
†Item not included in survey.
***$p < .05$; **$p < .10$.

constraints dictated that the joint influence of attributions and issue-specific opinions be examined serially, i.e., opinion by opinion (see appendix C).

Table 8.5 presents the results of parallel indirect effects analyses conducted with poverty, crime, terrorism, racial inequality, and the Iran-Contra affair. The table entries show, for each specific opinion, the percentage increase in that opinion's influence over general opinions among participants attributing causal and treatment responsibility to society (or to the president in the case of the Iran arms sale) (see appendix C). The entry of 33, corresponding to the interaction effect of societal causal attributions and presidential performance for poverty, indicates that the effects of this opinion on presidential popularity was increased by 33 percent when causal attributions for poverty were societal.

In every study, the analysis revealed that societal attributors assigned more weight to their issue-specific opinions than individualistic (or punitive) attributors when evaluating President Reagan's overall performance and character. The strongest evidence of such asymmetry was detected with crime and the Iran arms sale. In the case of the former, eleven of eighteen possible interaction effects between attributions and issue-specific opinions proved significant. Evaluations of the president's performance on crime, preferences concerning the level of government spending, and support for the death penalty all became more important as standards for evaluating the president when respondents offered societal attributions for crime. In the Iran-Contra study, when President Reagan was directly implicated in respondents' attributions, ratings of his foreign policy performance, preferences concerning government spending on anti-terrorist programs, and support for greater U.S. military involvement in Central America all became energized as criteria for general evaluations.

The same pattern was detected in the national survey. Ratings of President Reagan's performance concerning foreign policy performance exerted strengthened effects on ratings of his competence and evaluations of Vice President Bush when attributions for the arms sale were presidential. The evidence was especially striking for the Contra-aid issue. Among respondents who assigned responsibility to the president, support for Contra aid became a more powerful predictor of all four general evaluations by an average margin of nearly 50 percent. (Opponents of aid were less supportive of Reagan and Bush.) Similarly, when responsibility was assigned to the president, the per-

Table 8.5 Attribution of Responsibility and Evaluation of the President:
Indirect Effects

Poverty	Issue Performance		Government Spending		Social Services	
	Causal Resp.	Treatment Resp.	Causal Resp.	Treatment Resp.	Causal Resp.	Treatment Resp.
Overall performance	33***		33***		40****	
Competence	34**					
Integrity			100***		100****	

Crime	Issue Performance		Government Spending		Death Penalty	
	Causal Resp.	Treatment Resp.	Causal Resp.	Treatment Resp.	Causal Resp.	Treatment Resp.
Overall performance	9****	10****	83****	51***	55****	44**
Competence		37***	100****			65**
Integrity		42***		100**		

Terrorism	Issue Performance		Government Spending		Military Retaliation	
	Causal Resp.	Treatment Resp.	Causal Resp.	Treatment Resp.	Causal Resp.	Treatment Resp.
Overall performance		16**		38*		46***
Competence		35****		73****		73***
Integrity		33**		53**		66**

Racial inequality	Issue Performance		Government Spending		Help Minorities	
	Causal Resp.	Treatment Resp.	Causal Resp.	Treatment Resp.	Causal Resp.	Treatment Resp.
Overall performance	9*		100***	100**	100***	
Competence						
Integrity				78**		

continued

Table 8.5 *continued*

Iran arms sale (Suffolk County)	Issue Performance	Government Spending	Central America
	Causal Responsibility	Causal Responsibility	Causal Responsibility
Overall performance	22****	36***	44****
Competence	14*	38**	18*
Integrity	19****	63***	30***

Iran arms sale (CBS–NYT surveys)	Issue Performance	Iran-Contra Salience	Aid for Contras
	Causal Responsibility	Causal Responsibility	Causal Responsibility
Overall performance		30***	39**
Competence	8****	36***	42**
Integrity			33****
Evaluation of George Bush	10***	100***	75***

Notes: Table entries are the percentage increases in the effects of the predictor (column) variables on general evaluations among respondents attributing responsibility for the target issue to society. Blank entries indicate nonsignificant indirect effects coefficients. The number of cases for the indirect effects analyses ranges from 60 to 581.

****$p < .01$; ***$p < .05$; **$p < .10$; *$p < .15$.

ceived importance of the Iran-Contra issue had more influence on three of the four evaluations—the more important the issue, the more critical the evaluations.

Less clear-cut support for the indirect effects argument was obtained with respect to terrorism and poverty. Societal treatment (but not causal) attributions for terrorism boosted the effects of all three specific opinions on general evaluations. In the area of poverty, the pattern was reversed: causal attributions alone boosted the effects of the president's performance on poverty, preferences concerning government spending on defense, and support for social welfare services on evaluations of President Reagan's overall performance; however, these indirect effects appeared only sporadically when respondents rated the president's competence and integrity.

Finally, the indirect effects hypothesis fared poorly in the area of racial inequality. The only instance of attributions of responsibility increasing the influence of issue-specific opinions was the question on preferences for government spending; when treatment attributions were societal, these preferences were more influential in shaping all three presidential evaluations.

The special influence of societal attributions in affecting the interdependence of general and issue-specific opinions may reflect not only the "political" flavor of these attributions, but also the realities of the political situation. With Ronald Reagan in office, societal attributions of responsibility implied negative evaluations of the president, while other attributions implied positive evaluations. The power of societal attribution to enhance the influence of issue-specific opinions may therefore also reflect a "negativity bias" in political evaluations. There is evidence that negative traits or characteristics of politicians tend to exert stronger effects on voters' attitudes than positive traits or characteristics.[6] For individuals who attribute responsibility to society, issue-specific opinions are typically negative cues for evaluating President Reagan, and this may account, in part, for the pattern of results.

Conclusion

The several analyses of direct and indirect effects reported in this chapter indicate that citizens reward and punish presidents depending upon the manner in which they attribute responsibility for political issues. Over and above the effects of party affiliation and political ideology, President Reagan was held in lower esteem among individuals who attributed responsibility to society. The overall pattern of results suggests three generalizations about the degree to which attributions rub off on the public's image of the president.

First, the influence of attributions on presidential evaluations increases with issue salience. Of the issues examined in this study, crime was clearly the most salient (using either the total number of causes and treatments mentioned or responses to the "most important problems facing the nation" question as the measure of salience). Crime was also the only "ongoing" issue for which causal and treatment attributions both affected the president's public support.

A second thread running through the indirect and direct effects analyses concerns a divergence between issues of social welfare and issues of public security. In the case of social welfare issues, the direct effects of causal attributions overshadowed the direct effects of treatment attributions. In addition, societal causal attributions were more effective than societal treatment attributions in controlling the sensitivity of presidential evaluations to specific opinions.[7] For issues of public security, the opposite pattern held; societal causal attributions were secondary to societal treatment attributions in influencing, either directly or indirectly, presidential evaluations.[8] This difference may stem from stronger public expectations concerning the president as an agent of control with respect to issues of public security vis-à-vis issues of social welfare. The public may be more inclined to demand presidential action to control crime and terrorism but less inclined to do so when confronted with poverty or racial inequality.[9]

Attributions of treatment responsibility for terrorism may attach particularly closely to the president since the issue typically overlaps with foreign policy and national security concerns, which, both in reality and perception, are matters of executive prerogative. Jimmy Carter and Ronald Reagan both encountered their most severe public setbacks attempting to cope with terrorist threats and actions. In the case of President Carter, the Iranian hostage crisis, although initially a windfall in its "rallying" effect on his popularity, later forced the administration to attempt a military rescue that defied all odds: In Theodore Lowi's words:

> A peace-loving, religious man like Jimmy Carter did not take
> the risk of the Iranian rescue mission merely to give himself a
> convenient lever to move American public opinion. The
> leverage worked the other way: public opinion had forced upon
> the President an act of the sheerest adventurism.[10]

Ultimately, the hostage issue became President Carter's political albatross, contributing to widespread public perception of presidential weakness and electoral defeat at the hands of Ronald Reagan in 1980.

It was this very same burden of treatment responsibility for terrorism that ensnared the Reagan administration in the Iran-Contra debacle. Concerned that the president's policy of "talking tough" on terrorism (and bombing Libya on occasions) were not satisfying the public's expectations, the president's advisors embarked upon the bizarre policy of wooing the Iranian government with arms.

In addition to issue salience and the particular importance of treatment attributions for issues of public security, the influence of attributions on evaluations of the president depends upon an obvious point: the prominence of the president himself in citizens' attributions of responsibility. The issues of social welfare and public security examined here, although eliciting frequent societal attributions, were not marked by a particularly high concentration of presidential attributions. To attribute poverty to welfare programs that provide the poor with an insufficient incentive to work is a far cry from attributing poverty to specific steps taken by President Reagan. Given the complexity of most public issues and the division of governmental powers, presidents and their media advisors can induce citizens to discount the role of the president by citing a plethora of plausible alternative societal causes (most notably, the actions of Congress). More generally, through skilled media management, presidents can take or deny political responsibility, depending upon the political exigencies of the situation.[11]

In contrast to broad issues such as crime or poverty where people might cite a host of potential causes and treatments, other issues are, virtually by definition, matters of presidential attributions. Issues of national defense or diplomacy spotlight the public's attention on the president, as do the actions of the president's advisors and staff. Watergate, the Nixon pardon, the Iranian hostage crisis, and the Iran-Contra affair all epitomize the costs associated with such "presidential" issues. These are issues or events that pose strong threats to the president's popularity because they are characterized by few opportunities for discounting presidential responsibility; there was little President Reagan's media advisors could do but hope for the Iran-Contra issue to subside or for the networks to run more stories dealing with Middle East conflicts, for example. In sum, issues differ in their built-in relevance to evaluations of the president; long-standing issues can be attributed to societal agents other than the president. Specific decisions emanating from the White House make it difficult for the president to evade responsibility no matter how skilled his media managers.

NINE

The Role of Individual Differences

Thus far the analysis has documented the existence of network framing effects. The data show that attributions of causal and treatment responsibility are influenced by the presentation of television news in episodic or thematic frames and by particular subject matter emphases in the news.

This chapter examines individual differences in responsiveness to framing effects and variations in the generalizability of framing effects across issue areas. The evidence indicates that there are individual differences in suggestibility and that most viewers fail to generalize the impact of news frames across issues. For example, episodic framing of poverty has little impact on attributions of responsibility for unemployment.

Individual Differences in Susceptibility to Framing

This section considers the role of long-standing dispositional characteristics as mediators of network framing. The analysis will investigate the extent to which framing effects are limited or enhanced by "built-in" preferences for particular attributions. Three basic sets of dispositional characteristics are considered: partisanship, level of political involvement, and a residual category consisting of a number of social and demographic traits.

Partisanship is important because it captures the influence of early socialization and basic cultural values. The analysis of the interaction of partisanship and framing relies on the two major indicators of partisanship—party identification and liberal-conservative orientation (see appendix C). Both are known to be internalized at an early stage of life and to provide important filters for viewing political life.[1] As the analyses of specific and general opinions (reported in chapters 7 and 8) demonstrated, the opinion profiles of Democrats and Republicans and of liberals and conservatives differ consistently. Since partisans are more likely to have internalized a "belief system" that may include particular attributions of responsibility, the general expectation was that Democrats and Republicans would tend to differ in their responsiveness to particular news frames. Specifically, it was anticipated that Republicans would be more resistant than Democrats to thematic framing since their partisan sentiments dictate individualistic or punitive rather than societal attributions for the target issues under investigation. Conservatives were also expected to be less susceptible to thematic framing since societal attributions typically run counter to their ideology. In short, it was expected that partisanship would insulate viewers from inconsistent cues conveyed by news frames.

Levels of political involvement are also potentially significant as a resource for interpreting the news. People who are highly politically involved tend to know more about public issues, have access to more extensive and varied sources of information, and have more thought-out political interpretations; accordingly, they were expected to hold more firmly to their attributions of responsibility (whether societal or individualistic) in the face of countervailing contextual cues provided by television news reports than persons who were less politically involved. Put differently, the greater ability of the more involved viewer to counterargue with news stories was expected to produce a degree of immunity to framing effects.[2]

The various framing studies included questions tapping several dimensions of political involvement. These included political participation, political interest, information, and the frequency with which individuals watch television newscasts (see appendix C).

The final category of dispositional characteristics consisted of basic socioeconomic factors including education, race, gender, marital status, and age. These traits are known to be correlated with television usage. The less educated, minorities, housewives, the elderly, and females are more dependent upon television in general and television news in particular.[3] The degree to which network framing effects are strengthened (or weakened) by these characteristics is therefore suggestive of the extent of framing in the "real world."

The impact of the three types of dispositional characteristics (partisanship, political involvement, and socioeconomic background) was analyzed with respect to the issue areas of poverty, crime and terrorism (which were merged), and the Iran-Contra affair. Crime and terrorism were examined together because the relevant categories of causal and treatment attributions were identical in content. The two experiments for poverty were combined for purposes of this analysis.[4] Unemployment and racial inequality were both excluded from this phase of the analysis, the former because of the sheer weakness of the episodic versus thematic framing distinction and the latter because the experimental design incorporated a subject matter condition (racial discrimination) for which there was no episodic component.

For each of the three analyses, the experimental manipulation was simplified. In the cases of poverty and crime and terrorism, this meant pooling the various thematic and episodic conditions. In the case of the Iran-Contra study, this meant comparing the political framing conditions with the policy framing conditions.

Poverty, Crime, and Terrorism

The effects of dispositional characteristics on attributions for poverty and crime and terrorism are summarized in table 9.1. The table entries are average "adjusted responsibility scores" that indicate the relative tendency of any group to offer societal attributions in response to thematic framing. A positive score represents an increased tendency for the group in question to attribute responsibility to societal factors following exposure to thematic reports. In the case of Democrats, for instance, the entry of .20 for poverty causal attributions means that Democrats were significantly more likely to offer societal attributions in response to thematic framing of poverty than either Republicans or independents.[5]

For both causal and treatment attributions, partisanship was by far the most relevant characteristic. In effect, news reports suggesting societal responsibility for poverty, crime, or terrorism were rebuffed by Republicans and embraced by Democrats. In the case of crime and terrorism, the effects of political ideology mirrored those of party identification. Liberals were more responsive to thematic framing when attributing both causal and treatment responsibility, while conservatives were less responsive to thematic framing when consi-

Table 9.1 Individual Differences in Framing: Poverty, Crime, Terrorism

	Poverty[a]		Crime/Terrorism[b]	
	Causal Resp.	Treatment Resp.	Causal Resp.	Treatment Resp.
Partisanship				
Democrats	.20****	.12*		
Republicans	−.12****	−.17****	−.20***	−.33****
Independents				
Liberals	.07*		.12*	.24****
Conservatives				−.21***
Moderates				
Political involvement				
High participation				.21***
Low participation				−.09***
High interest	.13*			.11***
Low interest	−.05*			−.16***
High information				.19**
Low information				−.09**
Frequent news watchers				
Infrequent news watchers				
Personal background				
High education				
Low education				
White	−.03*			−.05***
Nonwhite	.20*			.37***
Males				
Females				
Age < 35			.20****	
Age > 35			−.16****	

Notes: Table entries are mean societal-attribution scores adjusted for the effects of thematic framing. Blank entries indicate nonsignificant differences between groups.
[a]$N = 330$.
[b]$N = 194$.
****$p < .01$; ***$p < .05$; **$p < .10$; *$p < .15$ by two-tailed t-test; e.g., Democrats differ from Republicans and independents at the .001 level of significance.

dering the question of treatment responsibility. The networks' influence was thus conditioned by long-standing partisan preferences.

With the exception of party identification and liberal-conservative placement, traces of individual differences were scarce. There was only one difference associated with political involvement for poverty—more interested viewers were more affected by thematic framing when attributing causal responsibility. A more pronounced pattern appeared for crime and terrorism; more interested, more informed, and more participant viewers were more responsive to thematic framing when attributing treatment responsibility. These results were counter to expectations in that framing effects tended to be strengthened rather than weakened among the more involved.

There were only a few individual differences associated with the indicators of personal background. Education and gender proved generally unrelated to the magnitude of framing; however, the treatment attributions of nonwhites were moved to a greater degree by thematic framing in both tests. Thematic framing of crime and terrorism exerted greater influence on the causal attributions of younger viewers.

The Iran-Contra Affair

The results of the individual-differences analysis for the Iran-Contra study are presented in table 9.2. The table entries show the degree to which groups were more or less likely to attribute responsibility to the president following exposure to political framing of the event. The entry of .29 for Democrats, for instance, indicates that compared with Republicans and independents, Democrats made presidential attributions more frequently after watching news reports that focused on the president's actions.

Given the results reported in chapter 8, it is not surprising that network framing effects were conditioned by viewers' party identification and ideological leanings. Democrats and liberals were more affected by news coverage suggesting presidential responsibility, while independents and conservatives were less affected.[6] In effect, viewers most likely to be habitually antagonistic toward President Reagan responded most readily to news reports that drew attention to the president as a causal agent.

Among the indicators of political involvement, the index of participation and the frequency with which individuals watched television news programs both influenced framing. Political activists and more frequent viewers of the news were less influenced by the dominant political frame. Once again, viewers' personal backgrounds were not reflected in differences in susceptibility to framing.

All told, the effects of network framing were conditioned mainly by

Table 9.2 Individual Differences
in Framing: The Iran-Contra Study

Partisanship	
Democrats	.29**
Republicans	
Independents	$-.17*$
Liberals	.50***
Conservatives	$-.39***$
Moderates	
Political involvement	
High participation	$-.12**$
Low participation	.30**
High interest	
Low interest	
High information	
Low information	
Frequent news watchers	$-.10*$
Infrequent news watchers	.16*
Personal background	
High education	
Low education	
Whites	
Nonwhites	
Males	
Females	
Age < 35	
Age > 35	
N	85

Notes: Table entries are mean presidential-attribution scores adjusted for the effects of political framing. Blank entries indicate nonsignificant differences between groups. ***$p < .01$; **$p < .05$; *$p < .10$ by two-tailed t-test.

long-standing partisan sentiments. Democrats and liberals were quick to respond to thematic reports, conservatives and Republicans to episodic reports. Similarly, Democrats and liberals were moved to a greater degree by political coverage of the Iran-Contra affair. These differences highlight the importance of partisan consistency to the attribution process. News reports suggesting particular attributions of responsibility are interpreted within a body of existing sentiments and preferences. When these suggestions are congruent with partisan sentiments, framing is augmented; when they clash, framing is weakened.

Do Network Framing Effects Spread?

To this point the analysis has only considered network framing within individual policy or issue areas. It is possible, however, that framing effects may spread across issues. Episodic framing of poverty, for instance, may influence how individuals attribute responsibility for unemployment and other related economic issues. In two experiments, the framing manipulations were designed to bear on both a primary and a secondary issue target, and measures of causal and treatment attributions were obtained for both issues. This arrangement permits two related tests of spillover in framing. The first test concerns the degree to which episodic or thematic framing of the primary target affects attribution of responsibility for the secondary target. The second test concerns the degree to which episodic or thematic framing influences between-issue consistency in viewers' causal and treatment attributions.[7]

Study 1: Poverty and Unemployment

Since poverty and unemployment both concern matters of economic security, it was hypothesized that individuals would answer questions of causal and treatment responsibility similarly; those who hold poor people responsible for poverty would also consider the unemployed responsible for their predicament. If the two issues are psychologically linked, thematic framing of poverty should strengthen attribution of societal responsibility for unemployment, while episodic framing of poverty should strengthen attribution of individual responsibility for unemployment.

Framing alternatives for poverty had little bearing on the direction in which individuals assigned responsibility for unemployment (see table 9.3). There was only one significant difference. Participants assigned to the thematic condition cited more societal causes of unemployment than participants assigned to the adult single mother condition ($p < .10$). In the area of treatment responsibility, there were no significant differences.

The results of the analysis suggest that individuals are rather stringent in what they take to be relevant information. Episodic and

Table 9.3 Spillover in Framing Effects: Poverty and Unemployment

Responsibility for Unemployment	Condition					
	Thematic (1)	Children (2)	Unemployed Worker (3)	Elderly Widow (4)	Adult Mother (5)	Teenage Mother (6)
Individual causal responsibility	.36	.38	.40	.28	.33	.25
Societal causal responsibility	.63*5	.54	.57	.56	.48	.56
Individual treatment responsibility	.24	.21	.22	.20	.13	.13
Societal treatment responsibility	.76	.74	.78	.80	.84	.86
N of subjects	49	43	38	39	49	26

Note: Table entries are mean attribution scores.
*differs at the .10 level by two-tailed t-test from the indicated condition.

thematic framing of poverty had little impact on attributions for unemployment. Framing effects did not generalize; the pattern of significant differences in viewers' attributions for poverty was not nearly reproduced in the case of unemployment.

To pursue further the question of spillover between the two issues, individual-level correlations between summary measures of causal and treatment responsibility were computed. Each respondent's percentage of individualistic attributions was subtracted from the percentage of societal attributions. The simple correlation (r) between these net responsibility scores for poverty and unemployment was .22 in the case of causal attributions and .26 in the case of treatment attributions. Despite the many surface similarities between unemployment and poverty, individuals did not attribute responsibility for these issues consistently. Moreover, neither episodic nor thematic framing of poverty had any effect on the level of inter-issue consistency; regardless of the news frame to which participants were exposed, attributions of responsibility tended to be issue-specific rather than common.

Study 2: Crime and Terrorism

In the unemployment-poverty comparison, only one of the issues (poverty) was the subject of the experimental framing manipulation.

In the study on crime and terrorism, both target issues were framed, thus permitting investigation of reciprocal effects. To the degree individuals attribute responsibility for crime and terrorism similarly, the framing effects induced by episodic or thematic reports within each issue area should also be manifest (albeit on a smaller scale) in the other; thematic framing of terrorism should strengthen societal attributions for crime, and episodic framing of crime should increase individualistic and punitive attributions for terrorism.

There was only one significant reciprocal effect of the crime and terrorism framing manipulations (table 9.4): Thematic framing of terrorism elicited a significantly higher level of societal treatment attributions for crime. While the level of societal attributions was .37

Table 9.4   Spillover in Framing Effects: Crime and Terrorism

	Coverage of Terrorism	
	Episodic	Thematic
Causal responsibility for crime		
Individual	.41	.42
Societal	.40	.41
Punitive	.17	.15
Treatment responsibility for crime		
Societal	.21*	.37
Punitive	.49	.42
N of subjects:	48	36

	Coverage of Crime	
	Episodic	Thematic
Causal responsibility for terrorism		
Individual	.36	.27
Societal	.45	.51
Punitive	.15	.10
Treatment responsibility for terrorism		
Societal	.30	.28
Punitive	.49	.51
N of subjects:	61	49

Note: Table entries are mean attribution scores.
*$p < .10$ by two-tailed t-test.

under conditions of thematic framing, it was only .21 under conditions of episodic framing. In all remaining categories of attributions, the distinction between episodic and thematic framing of crime made no difference to attributions for terrorism and vice versa.

Turning to the overall level of inter-issue consistency in attributions, the correlations between the indices of causal and treatment responsibility for the two issues were .20 and .31, respectively. The size of these correlations suggests that individuals connected crime and terrorism only loosely when attributing responsibility. Unlike the results from the poverty-unemployment experiment, however, the framing manipulations did affect the level of inter-issue consistency in attribution. Thematic framing of terrorism significantly increased the interdependence between both causal and treatment attributions, while thematic framing of crime significantly boosted the interdependence between treatment attributions for the two issues.[8] The results of this analysis thus suggest that under episodic framing viewers tended to keep their attributions of responsibility for crime and terrorism distinct; under thematic framing, however, their attributions became more convergent.

Overall, the framing effects tended to be issue-specific rather than general. More often than not, news frames influenced attributions of responsibility for a particular issue and did not carry over to related issues. The absence of spillover is especially telling because the comparisons reported here addressed issues that resembled each other closely. If news media framing of terrorism does not affect attributions for crime, it is not likely to affect attributions for more distant issues such as racial inequality or the cost of living.[9]

Conclusion

The analyses of individual differences and spillover reveal that the networks' ability to alter attributions of responsibility is limited. Individuals' partisan affiliations provide them an important resource with which to resist the suggestions of news frames. The influence of news stories is dependent upon correspondence or agreement between the suggestions conveyed by the news and more long-term cues conveyed by partisan affiliation. The political impact of network framing is also cushioned by the failure of the audience to generalize the implications of particular news frames to their attributions of responsibility for closely related issues.

Conclusion

Notwithstanding the inherent complexity of contemporary political life, ordinary citizens readily identify causes of national issues and suggest treatments or solutions for social problems. These attributions of causal and treatment responsibility are key factors in the formation of public opinion. The data reported here demonstrate that policy preferences, assessments of presidential performance, and evaluations of public institutions are all powerfully influenced by attributions of causal and treatment responsibility. Attributions and the political opinions they generate permit citizens to exercise political control, even though the public's level of factual knowledge is low.[1]

Individual respondents in the framing experiments tended to exhibit a low level of consistency across different issue areas in attributing responsibility to individual, societal, or other factors. This result suggests that people tend to consider political issues one by one, rather than developing an overarching schema for political responsibility; in other words, political thinking tends to be "domain specific."[2] The present data thus confirm the now classic findings of Converse and Lane that political belief systems are constricted rather than expansive and that members of any particular "issue public" tend to have dissimilar overall opinion profiles.[3] As Converse noted:

> A realistic picture of political belief systems in the mass public, then, is not one that omits issues and policy demands completely nor one that presumes widespread ideological coherence; it is rather one that captures with some fidelity the fragmentation, narrowness, and diversity of these demands.[4]

The unsatisfying result for scholars is that global opinion cues, though theoretically economical, perform poorly as predictors of issue-specific opinions, while more particularistic cues, though lacking in economy, offer strong explanatory leverage.

Attributions of responsibility can be seen as occupying a middle ground between the global and particularistic extremes. By reducing the complexity of political issues to the twin concepts of causation and treatment, attributions enable citizens to structure the otherwise dazzling array of events, policies, institutions, groups, and personalities that make up the day-to-day substance of national politics.

As discussed in the preceding chapters, television news frames play an important role in shaping attributions of political responsibility, although the impact of alternative frames was far from uniform across the various issue areas investigated. For example, for certain issue areas where the episodic news frame predominates, such as poverty and terrorism, episodic coverage tended to produce individualistic attributions without regard to the particular subject matter focus of the news stories. On the other hand, for the issue of crime, where episodic reporting is again the rule, episodic framing proved secondary in its effect on attributions to the particular subject matter under discussion. In other words, stories dealing with the issue of illegal drugs were likely to produce individualistic causal attributions, no matter how framed, while stories dealing with white crime were likely to produce societal causal attributions, no matter how framed.

The effects of alternative news frames also diverged for the two issues that received heavy thematic coverage—unemployment and racial inequality. Societal attributions prevailed for unemployment, even when the issue was framed episodically, and thus there were no framing effects for this issue. In the area of racial inequality, framing effects and the subject matter focus of the news both influenced attributions. Episodic framing of black poverty elicited a significantly higher frequency of individualistic attributions than did thematic framing; however, episodic and thematic coverage of affirmative action both produced predominantly societal attributions.

Finally, the alternative political and policy frames used to analyze the Iran-Contra affair were shown to influence attributions. The predominant political frame, which focused on the criticism and controversy surrounding the uncertain role of the president in the decision to sell arms to Iran, encouraged viewers to attribute causal responsibility to the president, while coverage that focused on the arms sale as an instrument of U.S. foreign policy tended to produce more contextual, nonpresidential attributions.

Before proposing a psychological explanation for the existence of media framing effects, some comments concerning the distinctiveness of the experimental evidence are in order. First, each study was carried out within a span of two hours. Therefore, no conclusion can be drawn concerning either the effect of repeated exposure to particular news frames or the rate at which framing effects decay.[5] Even if framing effects are transitory, however, they may nonetheless have a profound effect on outcomes that depend upon public opinion and behavior.

Second, the experimental manipulations involved only television news. The nature of the print media makes it likely that thematic framing will occur more frequently in newspaper and magazine articles than in television news stories. Therefore, if the participants in these experiments had been exposed to both television and newspaper coverage of issues, the influence of the predominant episodic frame in network news might have been attenuated (as probably happens to some extent in the real world).

The short time period spanned by the experiments and the absence of exposure to alternative news sources might suggest either that the evidence of media framing effects is exaggerated or understated. While it might be argued that the effects are exaggerated because of the immediacy of exposure, it is also true that a single two-minute story is a small stimulus in the context of a lifetime of political socialization. Seen in this light, it is perhaps remarkable that *any* framing effects were detected.

Moreover, all the target issues have either achieved "perennial" status in recent American history, or, in the case of the Iran-Contra affair, penetrated the consciousness of even the most apolitical American. Thus, the data were drawn exclusively from issues of high visibility. The consistent use of high visibility targets may provide a particularly stringent test of framing. People may be better equipped to formulate independent attributions of responsibility for these issues than for less familiar issues, and thus it would be reasonable to assume that people should be less susceptible to framing influences when the issue is highly familiar.

The Psychology of Media Effects

Dispositional versus Contextual Influence

Network framing effects occur within a psychological context. Cultural norms, party affiliation, personality traits, and other long-standing dispositional influences also affect attributions of responsibility. These political predispositions interact with network framing effects. For example, as discussed in chapter 9, episodic framing is more powerful in eliciting individualistic attributions for crime, terrorism, racial inequality, and poverty from Republicans and conservatives than from Democrats and liberals. In general, the greater the discrepancy between the attributions suggested by episodic or thematic framing and the viewer's predisposition, the weaker the influence of the news and vice versa.

Nevertheless, framing effects do occur regularly in the face of long-term personal predispositions. This finding casts doubt on the argument that cultural norms and political values are the paramount determinants of attributions of responsibility. The evidence presented here suggests a much more circumstantially bound process in which attributions also depend upon the prevailing winds of news coverage. While core values such as individualism and the work ethic do encourage people to hold individuals rather than governmental policies or societal conditions responsible for issues such as poverty or racial inequality, exposure to thematic news frames can and does override these predispositions.[6] More generally, the occurrence of network framing effects provides further confirmation of the inherently circumstantial nature of human judgment. Individuals' attributions of responsibility for political issues show significant short-term flux, depending upon the particular mix of thematic and episodic news frames in the everyday flow of information. Therefore, the conventional "dispositional" explanation of public opinion and political behavior that grants monopoly status to stable personal influences (most notably party affiliation, ideology, and personality traits) must be revised to allow for contextual influences.

The Accessibility Bias

The "accessibility bias" argument suggests that the influence of television news stems from its power to make information "accessible," or retrievable, from memory. In general, the theory is that information that can be more easily retrieved from memory tends to dominate judgments, opinions, and decisions, and that in the arena of public affairs, where people are highly dependent upon the media for information, more accessible information is information that is more frequently or more recently conveyed by the media.

Obviously, any number of factors and criteria could be considered in forming an impression of a person, purchasing a product, or choosing between political candidates, vacation tours, or job offers. The accessibility bias assumes that individuals tend to retrieve only a tiny sample of information from long-term memory. Rather than ransacking their memories for every piece of relevant information, individuals select information that happens to be more conveniently "located" or accessible.

There are several competing accounts of the memory structures and processes that determine accessibility of particular information or considerations. Wyer and Srull, for example, propose a model of long-term memory in which items of information are categorized and stored in a series of "referent bins" (bins containing subject matter information about particular politicians, issues, events, or groups). A critical postulate of the Wyer and Srull model is that those items of information that have been more frequently (or recently) used are stacked at the top of the referent bins and are therefore encountered first when individuals locate the appropriate bin.[7]

The reliance on more accessible information is a particular instance of the well-known human proclivity to simplify. From Simon's pioneering work on "satisficing" to Tversky and Kahneman's "cognitive heuristics," the common denominator of psychological research into judgment and decision making has been the dominance of intuitive and informal over rigorous and systematic approaches to decision or choice problems. People search for strategies that economize effort and are simple to apply and settle for acceptable rather than optimal strategies. As Slovic, Fischhoff, and Lichtenstein have described this general tendency,

> people solve problems, including the determination of their
> own values, with what comes to mind. The more detailed,
> exacting and creative their inferential process, the more likely
> they are to think of all they know about the problem. The
> briefer that process becomes, the more they will be controlled
> by the relative accessibility of various considerations.[8]

Simplification strategies should also be expected in the arena of politics where so few citizens are prepared to be detailed, exacting, and creative.

The accessibility bias has been documented thoroughly in experiments by social psychologists. These studies typically measure the weights that people assign to various considerations when expressing attitudes or making choices. Considerations that were made more accessible (by a variety of experimental methods) were found to exert significantly greater effects on attitudes and choices than competing considerations that were equally relevant (on objective terms), but were less accessible in the particular experimental context.[9]

Well-known manifestations of the differential-weighting-by-accessibility principle include the tendency to overestimate the importance of sensationalized events (such as fires and traffic accidents) as causes of death and to underestimate the importance of "quiet" risks such as heart disease and stroke.[10] Identical results have been obtained with respect to interpersonal impressions; people evaluate their friends or colleagues by reference to traits or features that are momentarily prominent.[11] Social psychologists have also shown that attitudes, like information, may be made more or less accessible and that the more accessible the attitude, the higher the degree of attitude-behavior consistency.[12]

In the world of politics, where people must rely heavily on the media for information, patterns of news coverage are critical determinants of accessibility. Typically, what comes to mind when the citizen thinks about public affairs are the images and information that flash across the television screen. Of course, accessibility is also determined by individual characteristics such as party affiliation, socioeconomic status, cultural values, religious upbringing, or the intensity of particular attitudes. For example, some individuals will habitually retrieve information about current economic conditions when attributing responsibility for poverty, no matter how extensively the media frame the issue in episodic terms.

In addition to the framing effects that are the subject of this work, political scientists have identified three major manifestations of the accessibility bias in public opinion: agenda-setting effects, priming effects, and "bandwagon" effects in political campaigns. The well-known "agenda-setting" effect refers to the tendency of people to cite issues "in the news" when asked to identify the significant problems facing the nation. Agenda-setting effects have been observed for all forms of mass media coverage, in experimental studies that have physically manipulated the extent of news coverage, and in survey-based studies that have tracked news coverage and issue salience over time. These studies employed both open-ended questions in which respondents identified the "most important problems facing the country" and closed-ended items in which they ranked the importance of particular issues. These agenda-setting effects have been observed for both local and national "problems." In all these areas, research has shown that individuals habitually refer to issues or events that have recently commanded extensive news coverage.[13]

The so-called "priming effect" refers to the ability of news programs to affect the criteria by which individuals judge their political leaders. Specifically, researchers have found that the more prominent an issue is in the national information stream, the greater will be the weight accorded it in making political judgments. While agenda-setting reflects the impact of news coverage on the perceived importance of national issues, priming refers to the impact of news coverage on the weight assigned to specific issues in making political judgments. For instance, after watching news stories on the increased budgetary outlays for the Pentagon under the Reagan administration, viewers were not only more likely to cite the arms race as an important national issue, but were also likely to give more weight to their evaluations of President Reagan's performance on arms control when rating his performance overall.[14]

The priming effect has been established in several experiments for evaluations of both presidents and congressmen, with news coverage of both political accomplishments and failures and across a wide range of issue areas. Priming effects have also been observed in assessments of political leaders' competence and integrity.[15] Significant priming effects have also been detected in data from national surveys. In a recent study, for example, Krosnick and Kinder found that Americans' opinions toward U.S. support for the Nicaraguan Contras and their support for U.S. intervention in Central America became *twice as influential* as determinants of President Reagan's popularity in the period immediately following the disclosure that funds from the sale of arms to Iran had been used to finance the Contras.[16]

The final illustration of the accessibility bias in the media-effects literature concerns the phenomenon of momentum, or campaign "bandwagons." Recent analyses have centered on the effects of "horse race" reporting in the making and unmaking of American presidential candidates. These news stories, which have become a staple of campaign coverage, detail the candidates' electoral prospects—their poll standings, delegate counts, fund-raising efforts, and related campaign indicators—rather than the candidates' policy positions or personal characteristics.[17]

The accessibility bias suggests that such reporting tends to cause the public to think about candidates in terms of their electoral viability and thus has the potential to create a bandwagon effect. For instance, Bartels reports that virtually all Democrats interviewed after the 1984 New Hampshire primary who had heard of Gary Hart offered an opinion on his prospects for gaining the nomination; however, only a tiny minority could offer an opinion concerning Hart's position on the major campaign issue of the day (cuts to federal social programs).[18] Clearly, electoral viability was a more visible feature of Gary Hart's candidacy than his position on major public issues. Of course, perceptions of the candidates' relative electoral strength are significantly colored by voters' preferences; in effect, voters engage in wishful thinking and tend to overestimate the chances of the candidates they like.[19] Researchers have found, however, that horse-race coverage modifies perceptions of electoral viability and thereby indirectly alters voting preferences, providing a strong favorable impetus toward the candidates whose prospects appear brightest.[20]

Framing effects can also be understood in terms of the accessibility bias. Episodic reporting tends to make particular acts or characteristics of particular individuals more accessible, while thematic reporting helps viewers to think about political issues in terms of societal or political outcomes. The survey evidence on framing (reported in chapter 2) suggests that accessibility may be affected by question format and wording. Thus, people describe themselves as disinterested in politics if they are first asked a series of difficult factual questions concerning the identity and activities of various public officials. On the other hand, if they are asked about their political interest before being confronted with the factual-knowledge questions, they describe themselves as substantially interested.[21] Similarly, questions that probe attitudes toward "people on welfare" may make concepts such as "waste" or "handout" more accessible, while questions that refer to "poor people" may activate concepts of "need" and "suffering." Thus, by stimulating the accessibility of differing conceptual frameworks, the terms of the survey questionnaire may themselves affect attributions of responsibility.[22]

These various illustrations of the accessibility bias substantiate Walter Lippmann's famous observation that the "pictures in peoples' heads" determine their political choices. The exercise of enlightened citizenship demands that the complexity of public affairs be somehow overcome, and these "pictures" are certainly a convenient basis for doing so. Inevitably the question arises whether voters acting in accordance with pictures in their heads—pictures put there by news coverage—arrive at the same political outcome as would voters endowed with perfect information and "detailed, exacting, and creative" choice processes.

One possibility is that media-induced accessibility effects will deflect individuals from their personal concerns and needs. The focus of television news coverage on national issues or events, which ordinarily are of secondary personal importance, means that voters may pay more attention to national issues than they would in the absence of such coverage (e.g., given voters' natural, self-oriented interests). This may account for the surprising phenomenon that voters' decisions are affected more by perceptions of national conditions than by immediate personal circumstances (the so-called "sociotropic" voting phenomenon). Thus Kinder and Kiewiet (1979) have found that voters weigh their assessments of the state of the national economy more heavily than assessments of their personal economic circumstances when evaluating political candidates.[23]

Presumably, the tendency of the media to enhance the accessibility of national issues and diminish the influence of personal problems on voting decisions strengthens the democratic process, although any such social benefits deriving from media attention to national issues would be tempered by biases in the selection of the particular issues to be covered. Unfortunately, the media news agenda is heavily influenced by political leaders and their "handlers." It is unlikely that the actions of Willie Horton or Governor Dukakis's drive in a tank would have engaged the networks were it not for the "media management" strategies of the 1988 Bush campaign.[24] More generally, as Petrocik has pointed out, political parties prefer to campaign over issues that, historically, have worked to benefit their candidates.[25] Democrats and Republicans thus differ in the issues they seek to inject into political campaigns.

Not only do campaign operatives and their clients impart a particular issue emphasis to news reports, but television news is also subject to a plethora of editorial influences including organizational norms (such as the tendency to mimic "leading" newspapers) and commercial imperatives (such as the need for good ratings).[26] The correspondence between television news coverage and political "reality" is thus inevitably loose.[27] Voters are led down pathways of judgment defined by news makers and their partisan biases or by the internal dynamics of news organizations. In addition to potential biases that impinge on editorial judgments of newsworthiness, the pervasiveness of the episodic frame in television newscasts is itself a significant source of distortion in the democratic process. The remaining discussion considers the implications of this journalistic practice for citizens' understanding of the political world.

Political Implications of Episodic Framing

The most striking feature of media framing effects is their remarkable specificity. The single instance in the experimental data of framing effects spilling over to a related issue concerned crime and terrorism. People who viewed episodic coverage of terrorism tended to produce fewer societal attributions for crime. (Of course, for many people, terrorism may be but a particular manifestation of "crime.") For other issue areas, framing effects simply do not generalize. This result is yet another manifestation of the much-documented absence of general, "ideological" reasoning among ordinary citizens.[28]

Americans' failure to see interconnections between issues may be a side effect of episodic news coverage. Most would agree that social problems such as poverty, racial inequality, drug usage, and crime are related in cause and treatment. Yet television typically depicts these recurring political problems as discrete instances and events. This tendency may obscure the "big picture" and impede the process of generalization. The results reported in chapter 9 included only three instances of framing having any effect on the consistency of attributions between issues. It is revealing that all of these cases involved less consistency under episodic framing (relative to thematic framing). Thus, episodic framing of crime or terrorism weakened the connections between attributions for crime and terrorism. In short, television news may contribute to domain specificity in political reasoning. Like the networks' dominant episodic news frame, Americans' perspective on political problems tends to be concrete rather than abstract and specific rather than general.

By simplifying complex issues to the level of anecdotal evidence, television news leads viewers to issue-specific attributions of responsibility, and these attributions tend to shield society and government from responsibility. Following exposure to episodic framing, Americans describe chronic problems such as poverty and crime not in terms of deep-seated social or economic conditions, but as mere idiosyncratic outcomes. Confronted with a parade of news stories describing particular instances or illustrations of national issues, viewers focus on individual and group characteristics rather than historical, social, political, or other such structural forces. In this respect episodic framing encourages reasoning by resemblance—people settle upon causes and treatments that "fit" the observed problem.

Americans are not, however, intrinsically averse to structural or systemic accounts of responsibility for issues. When television news coverage presents a more general or analytic frame of reference for national problems, the public's reasoning about causal and treatment responsibility shifts accordingly. Following exposure to news reports about increases in malnutrition nationwide, poverty becomes a matter of inadequate social welfare programs; confronted with news accounts of the shrinking demand for unskilled labor, unemployment becomes a matter of shortsighted economic policies or insensitive public officials; provided with news reports on deteriorating conditions in the inner cities, individual cite increased economic opportunities for the underprivileged as the appropriate remedy for crime, and so on.

In its principal effect, therefore, the dominant episodic news frame illustrates what some media scholars and critics have termed the "hegemonic" model of public communication. In this model, the dissemination of information is considered part of an elaborate "code control" process through which existing power structures are maintained. That is, news organizations in general and television in particular tend to be spokesmen for dominant groups and their ideology.[29]

Not only does episodic framing divert attention from societal responsibility, but, because attributions of responsibility prove to be such potent opinion cues, network news also tends to preserve the image of public officials (at least those who are not the subject of scandal). Television is thus a significant resource for political elites; event-oriented and case study news coverage effectively insulates incumbent officials from any rising tide of disenchantment over the state of public affairs.

This "proestablishment" effect of television news is counter intuitive: journalists, political analysts, and social psychologists all tend to
assume that the tendency of network news to personalize national issues represents a particularly vivid and powerful means of attacking
the president and the administration.[30] Depictions of hungry children, drug-related slayings, laid-off workers, or terrorist bombings
are thought to encourage the public to blame the president. President Reagan's criticism of network news in the midst of the 1982
recession typifies this fear.

> You can't turn on the evening news without seeing that they're
> going to interview someone else who has lost his job. Is it news
> that some fellow out in South Succotash has just been laid off
> and that he should be interviewed nationwide? (Interview with
> *The Daily Oklahoman,* 16 March 1982)

The results reported here, however, indicate rather that presidential
advisors should actively encourage "South Succotash" stories. Instead of raising questions about presidential responsibility, these
stories have precisely the opposite effect.[31]

While the main effect of the networks' predominant episodic frame
is to strengthen the legitimacy of officialdom, the effect is apparently
fortuitous. The motivation for the widespread use of episodic framing
concerns matters of organizational routine, format, and marketing
rather than partisan or ideological agendas. Journalistic norms such
as "objectivity" place a premium on the reporting of "hard" news such
as specific events. Interpretive, "subsurface" reporting is much more
vulnerable to charges of bias and editorializing.[32] Moreover, within
the constraints of a twenty-two minute "headline service," in-depth,
analytic, or interpretive reports on national issues would leave little
room for other news items. Finally, there is the all-powerful commercial imperative; audience ratings points and the advertising dollar are
critical. Episodic reporting, which typically features "good pictures,"
is likely to attract and keep viewers' attention. Thematic reporting, on
the other hand, tends to be dull and slow-paced, characteristics that
are not likely to strengthen viewer interest. The distinguished schol-
ar of American journalism Ben H. Bagdikian has argued that the
commercial dictates of news programming represent the root cause
for the prominence of the episodic frame in American public affairs
journalism. In discussing concentrated corporate control over news
organizations, Bagdikian identifies several consequences for news

programming, including the distinctive episodic nature of American news programs.

> What is weak in U.S. journalism, compared to the best journalism in other democracies, is systematic political and social analysis that indicates the sources, relationship, and consequences of individual events.[33]

In short, there are powerful organizational pressures that lead television news reporters and editors to seize upon specific events and particular episodes for representing political issues.

Journalistic norms and practices do not mean that presidents and other officials can always count on episodic framing for protection from accountability. During outbursts of prolonged political controversy, events become more spontaneous, and the White House is no longer in a position to orchestrate the news. Under these "crisis," circumstances, the networks assert their prerogatives of independence. Two-thirds of the network news reports on the Iran arms sale dwelled on political opposition to the decision. As the results in chapter 6 revealed, these news reports directed viewers to attributions of presidential responsibility and brought about a precipitous dip in President Reagan's popularity. Such instances of adversarial reporting, if sufficiently frequent, can inflict significant damage on any president's political standing. The ability to stave off these "media crises" is hence a critical political skill. Once a crisis erupts, however, the damage to the president's image can be minimized by framing the controversy as a matter of disagreement over government policy rather than disagreement over the president's ability to lead. When the networks covered Iran-Contra developments in light of the Iran-Iraq war or the fate of U.S. hostages in the Middle East, viewers became less likely to hold the president personally responsible.

The power of television news frames to influence attributions of responsibility for national issues also has important policy implications. To the degree that Americans do *not* hold society responsible for political issues, they are less apt to favor governmental initiatives or efforts to address these issues. For example, when individuals hold society responsible for poverty, they favor active governmental efforts to assist the poor. The results reported here suggest that the framing of social welfare issues in terms of particular categories of individuals or groups will weaken rather than strengthen public support for welfare. Yet ever since the New Deal, social welfare policy in this country has been formulated in terms of programs that target specific beneficiary groups, such as children, the disabled, single mothers, or the elderly. The identical argument can be made with respect to terrorism. U.S. responses to terrorist actions have invariably taken a "case-by-case" approach and have been targeted at specific nations or groups. The Reagan administration, for instance, published a list of countries that sponsored terrorists (including Iran) and recommended a variety of economic and commercial sanctions against them. By repeatedly defining the problem in terms of specific perpetrators, people become more concerned with measures to capture and punish terrorists rather with measures designed to address the more deep-seated social and economic issues that prompt the formation of terrorist organizations. Stated more generally, the use of a particularistic (or group-specific) as opposed to universalistic definition of political problems is a potent persuasive tool for elites who seek to curtail the role of government as an agent of social or economic change. As Gamson has argued, by circumscribing the national debate over public policy, episodic framing is a powerful form of social control.[34]

All told, the evidence on network framing provides another dimension to the "organization process" view of mass media influence. Routine decisions concerning the gathering and presentation of news impose a highly restricted range of perspectives on public issues.[35] Rather than providing a "marketplace of ideas," television provides only a passing parade of specific events, a "context of no context."[36] Because reasoning about responsibility is influenced by news frames, and because the episodic frame predominates, the upshot is that instead of serving as a restraining force on political elites, television further legitimizes their pronouncements and actions.[37]

Episodic Framing and Political Accountability

The ability of citizens to exercise control over the actions of their elected representatives is generally regarded as *the* critical measure of democratic government. According to the theory of "retrospective voting," the public exerts its influence essentially by approving or rejecting the performance of incumbents, rather than by selecting between the competing campaign platforms and promises of the contestants.[38] The fear of punishment at the polls ostensibly forces politicians to address the nation's problems by enacting legislation that is expected to benefit constituents. The logic of retrospective voting assumes, however, that voters can and will attribute responsibility for national problems to government. If voters fail to attribute responsibility to their leaders, elected officials have no incentive to address difficult issues and may with impunity substitute slogans and aphorisms for programs and arguments.

Ideally, the mass media in a democratic society should furnish a "mirror image" of political reality, and should assist viewers in seeing the connections between governmental actions (or inactions) and social problems. For a number of reasons, however, American network news fails to live up to this ideal. As has been frequently observed, the time constraints on news programming dictate that many issues will be effectively excluded from consideration. In addition, commercial realities and norms of journalistic objectivity have prompted the networks to cast their coverage of most major issues in episodic terms.

The premium placed on episodic framing means that many issues of significance have not received and will not receive the news coverage necessary to permit the public to become critical observers of national affairs. Many social problems tend to be invisible because they lack immediate or readily traceable symptoms. These subjects have been deemed less newsworthy by journalists hungry for "good pictures." For example, deficiencies in public education, the emergence of a large and seemingly permanent underclass, and gradual environmental degradation do not typically manifest themselves as specific events, and stories on these issues are infrequent. Similarly, the corruption in and mismanagement of savings and loan institutions failed to attract media attention until politicians were forced to acknowledge the true impact of the losses on the federal budget.

The present work suggests that television news not only fails as a mirror of political reality, but also operates in a systematic fashion to shape viewers' attributions of responsibility for political affairs in a way that tends to undermine the democratic norm of electoral accountability. The experiments reported here show that exposure to episodic framing tends to elicit individualistic (or nonsocietal) attributions of responsibility for most of the issues studied. Obviously, effective responses to most if not all of these problems will require concerted, programmatic assaults, which can best be launched with the support, and in some cases, the direct involvement, of government. Because television news generally fails to activate (and may indeed depress) societal attributions of responsibility, however, it tends to obscure the connections between social problems and the actions or inactions of political leaders. By attenuating these connections, episodic framing impedes electoral accountability.

The failure of recent administrations to deal with pressing issues is symptomatic of the breakdown of electoral accountability in American politics. Even conservative critics such as Kevin Phillips, who generally favor a limited role for government, have condemned government's "frightening inability to define and debate America's emerging problems."[39] Other observers of the Washington scene have also complained about paralysis and governmental irresponsibility. In the words of *The New Yorker* correspondent Elizabeth Drew, "The state of our politics is such now that there is no reward for being responsible, or for facing hard questions."[40] Clearly, the United States needs leaders with the ability to confront public problems and to take the associated political risks.

Nowhere is the debilitating influence of episodic framing on political accountability more apparent than in presidential election campaigns. The tendency to reduce a political campaign to daily ten-second "sound bites,"[41] and the unending focus on the horse race or the mechanics of the contest guarantee that coverage of the issues and the candidates' policy proposals will receive minimal attention. Superficial coverage of campaigns is a powerful disincentive for candidates to take national issues seriously. When the Dukakis campaign issued a series of detailed proposals designed to protect middle-income familes from the skyrocketing costs of college tuition, these proposals were virtually ignored by the networks.[42]

Instead of forcing the candidates to address the issues of clear social or economic significance, television news coverage of the 1988 campaign focused on the Pledge of Allegiance, patriotism, prison-furlough programs, flag desecration, membership in the American Civil Liberties Union, and other issues more symbolic than substantive. Moreover, when the candidates did address issues of substance, their rhetoric and arguments were far from compelling. George Bush committed himself to an "education presidency" while simultaneously, and seemingly inconsistently, opposing tax increases; Michael Dukakis attributed Massachusetts's economic growth in the 1980s entirely to his superior leadership skills. Summing up their impressions of the victorious Bush campaign, the veteran journalists Jack W. Germond and Jules Witcover noted that the campaign process in general, and patterns of television news coverage in particular, "enabled Bush to finesse the truly serious issues facing the country, setting up a smokescreen behind which he was able to speak in vacuous generalities about 'values' and avoid programmatic specifics that voters had a right to expect."[43]

In the long run, episodic framing contributes to the trivialization of public discourse and the erosion of electoral accountability. Because of its reliance on episodic reporting, television news provides a distorted depiction of public affairs. The portrayal of recurring issues as unrelated events prevents the public from cumulating the evidence toward any logical, ultimate consequence. By diverting attention from societal and governmental responsibility, episodic framing glosses over national problems and allows public officials to ignore problems whose remedies entail burdens to their constituents. Television news may well prove to be the opiate of American society, propagating a false sense of national well-being and thereby postponing the time at which American political leaders will be forced to confront the myriad economic and social ills confronting this society.

Appendix A
Content Analysis

Coding

The procedures used to code the news stories and the survey are
described below.

All of the news stories were coded by two independent student
coders who were unaware of the researcher's objectives. Coding reliability was assessed by computing the percentage of consistent
classifications. This percentage of inter-coder agreement ranged from
93 in the case of poverty to 82 in the case of the Iran arms sale. Dis-
agreements were resolved by submitting the story in question to a
third coder.

All of the survey questions, designed to elicit attributions of causal
and treatment responsibility, were coded independently by either
two or three graduate-student coders. Across all six issues examined
in this research, the average level of inter-coder agreement was approximately .90 for both causal and treatment responsibility.

Corroborating Textual and Visual Analyses

Very few news stories were exclusively thematic or episodic. The
either-or classification used here, however, does not represent a significant distortion, because the typical news story, though including
elements of both frames, was clearly tilted in one direction or the
other. To validate the classification of stories based on the *Abstracts*, a
visual examination of news coverage was undertaken for terrorism,

poverty, and unemployment. A representative sample of 52 CBS stories on terrorism was viewed. Of these, 80 percent were primarily episodic and 20 percent were primarily thematic. Stories classified as episodic, on average, devoted 83 percent of their airtime to episodic coverage, while the stories classified as thematic devoted an average of 80 percent of their airtime to thematic coverage.

All of the identified CBS stories on poverty were viewed. Poverty stories that were classified as thematic on the basis of the *Abstracts* devoted, on average, 89 percent of their airtime to thematic framing. For stories classified as episodic, the proportion of episodic time averaged 82 percent. A large sample of the CBS stories on unemployment were viewed. The comparable averages for the unemployment sample were 80 percent for stories classified as thematic and 85 percent for stories considered episodic. In short, typical CBS stories on terrorism, poverty, and unemployment mixed thematic and episodic framing sparingly; stories tended to tilt clearly in the direction of one or the other of the two frames. Put differently, there were hardly any stories in which episodic and thematic framing were evenly represented.

Appendix B
Field Experiments

The nine experiments were administered between June 1985 and September 1987. The number of individuals participating in the experiments ranged from 40 to 244. The location, scheduling of viewing sessions, and experimental procedures were the same in every experiment.

Measuring Attributions of Causal and Treatment Responsibility

For each respondent, the number of responses to the open-ended questions that referred to particular categories of causal and treatment responsibility was divided by the total number of responses. The measure of societal causal responsibility for poverty, for instance, was the proportion of causal responses citing societal conditions and governmental actions/inactions. Similarly, the measure of punitive treatment responsibility for crime and terrorism was the proportion of treatment responses calling for the imposition of stronger penalties.

These measures reflect the relative frequency of particular attributions. Two alternative indicators, corresponding to absolute frequency, were also constructed. The first was the sheer number of causal and treatment responses referring to societal, individualistic, or punitive responsibility. The second was a simple dichotomy in which respondents who mentioned at least one societal, individualistic, or punitive attribution were compared with respondents who mentioned none. The results based on these alternative indicators, while generally similar to the results based on the proportional measures, indicated somewhat stronger framing effects.

Identifying Models of Responsibility

The various models of responsibility were identified by cross-tabulating "net" causal and treatment responsibility scores. These scores reflect the relative predominance of societal over individualistic attributions (in the case of poverty, unemployment, and racial inequality), and of societal over individualistic and punitive attributions in the case of crime and terrorism. Thus a person who mentioned two societal causes of unemployment and one individual cause received a score of net score of $+.34$ ($.67 - .33$). Similarly, a person who mentioned only societal causes of unemployment received a score of 1, while a person who mentioned only individual factors received a score of -1. In the particular case of racial inequality, the percentage of causal and treatment attributions referring to affirmative action or preferential treatment were added to the percentage of individualistic attributions and subtracted from the percentage of societal attributions. These net scores were dichotomized at the zero point.

In the case of attributions of causal responsibility for crime and terrorism, the percentage of responses that cited individuals' character and inadequate punishment (individual and punitive responsibility) were summed and then subtracted from the percentage that cited societal conditions. The resulting difference score was dichotomized at the zero point. In the case of treatment responsibility, the percentage of "stronger punishment" responses (punitive responsibility) was subtracted from the percentage of "improved social conditions" responses (societal responsibility), and the resulting difference score was dichotomized.

Statistical Significance

The concept of statistical significance refers to the reliability of observed differences. A statistically significant difference is one that, theoretically, would emerge repeatedly were the same experiment to be run over and over. A difference that is significant at the .05 level (referred to in the figures and tables as $p < .05$) is one that would appear ninety-five times out of one hundred; a difference that meets the .10 level can be expected ninety times, and so on. Generally, statistical significance is more difficult to observe when the number of observations (i.e., study participants) is relatively small. It is also more difficult to attain significant differences when the researcher used "nondirectional" or two-tailed tests of significance. Given the small size of the experimental conditions and the use of two-tailed significance tests throughout (despite strong directional expectations in several instances that would have warranted the use of more generous one-tailed tests), the significance tests reported here are *inherently conservative.*

Poverty Experiment 2

A capsule description of each condition is given below.

In the Black Child condition, a black boy and girl living in a St. Louis child-care institution described their aspirations for the future, and social worker commented on the severity of child poverty. In the corresponding White Child condition, two brothers described what they eat every day, and the reporter noted their lack of toys. A social worker commented on the severity of child poverty.

In the White Unemployed Worker condition, a Wisconsin man described the several cost-cutting measures his family has had to resort to. The reporter noted the bleak economic prospects in the region. In the corresponding Black Unemployed Worker condition, an unemployed Vietnam veteran lamented the lack of employment opportunities for a person without special skills, and the director of a local employment agency described the shortage of blue-collar job openings.

In the White Adult Single Mother condition, the report portrayed a mother in her thirties who described the suddenness of her divorce and the difficulties (both monetary and psychological) of being on welfare. In the Black Adult Single Mother condition, a woman in her thirties described her difficulties in locating affordable housing and decent child care and expressed the hope that she will be able to work at some point.

In the Retired Widow conditions, the news story portrayed either a black or white woman on social security (both in their sixties) who described their financial difficulties and their fears that social security benefits would fail to keep pace with the cost of living.

Finally, both Teenage Single Mother conditions began with the anchor's statement that teens represent a growing percentage of single parents in America. The white condition featured a teenager with one baby. The mother indicated that the father of the child had denied parental responsibility but that her family was able to provide social and emotional support. The counterpart black teenager (also with one baby) stated that she had been forced to drop out of high school but that she hoped to return and graduate as soon as possible.

Appendix C
Correlational Analysis

Survey Indicators

Personal Characteristics

Political party affiliation was measured using the standard closed-ended question, i.e., "Generally speaking, do you consider yourself a Republican, a Democrat, an Independent, or what?" Dummy (dichotomous) variables were then constructed corresponding to respondents who indicated a Republican or Democratic preference on the party identification question. Liberal-conservative placement was assessed along a seven-point scale, the end points of which were labelled "strongly liberal" (1) and "strongly conservative" (7). Participants choosing responses 1 or 2 were classified as liberal while those selecting 6 or 7 were classified as conservative. The various correlational analyses were also run with the "full form" of the party identification and ideology questions; in no case were the results noticeably different.

Political activity was operationalized with a four-item index. Respondents were asked whether they had voted in the past presidential election, had contributed money to a political organization or candidate, had worked for a campaign, or had attended a political rally or meeting. Responses to these questions were scored 0 or 1 (corresponding to no/yes answers) and then summed.

Interest in politics was tapped with three questions. Respondents indicated how often they discussed "politics and public affairs" with people they knew, how often they "follow what's going on in government," and how much attention they "usually give" to news about government and politics. These three questions were invariably highly intercorrelated and were summed to form an index of political interest.

Political information was defined in issue-specific terms. That is, in any particular experiment, participants' information scores reflect information about the issues or issues under investigation. In the case of poverty, for example, respondents were asked to indicate the national poverty rate, the direction in which the size of the federal budget deficit had changed under President Reagan, the direction in which governmental social welfare expenditures had changed under President Reagan, and the group of Americans for whom the poverty rate was highest.

A single question was used to gauge frequency of news watching: "How often do you watch the national news on TV: hardly ever, once or twice a week, three or four times a week, almost every day?"

Finally, the specific economic indicators were respondents' level of education and their race.

Issue-specific Opinions

Poverty

Evaluations of President Reagan's budget and performance concerning poverty were made on a five-point scale that ranged from "very good" to "very poor." Evaluations of business leaders were made on a five-point scale that ranged from "helped decrease poverty significantly" to "helped worsen poverty significantly." The government-spending questions for defense and social welfare services were in the form of seven-point scales ranging from "greatly increase spending" to "greatly decrease spending." The question on defense spending was treated as relevant to poverty because many people view defense and social welfare expenditures as trade-offs. In fact, responses to the two questions were strongly (and negatively) correlated.

The counterpart measures in the NES Pilot survey were as follows: evaluations of President Reagan's handling of "the balancing of the national budget" (v5441) and "the economy" (v8414); an index of support for increased government spending on social welfare programs (social security, programs that help blacks, medicare, and child care), support for "government-guaranteed jobs" (v707) and "government help to minorities" (v714); feeling thermometer ratings of poor people (V5219), welfare recipients (V5228), and black people (V8118).

The items from the NES Pilot Survey measuring societal causal responsibility were variables 8240–43. Respondents were asked to agree or disagree (using a five-point scale) with the following potential causes: "low wages in some businesses and industries," "failure of society to provide good schools for many Americans," "prejudice and discrimination against blacks," and "failure of private industry to provide enough jobs." The items tapping individual responsibility consisted of variables 8235–38: "lack of effort by the poor," "lack of thrift and poor money management by poor people," "loose morals and drunkenness," and "lack of ability and talent among poor people." The average item intercorrelation for the societal items (r) was .34; for the individualistic items the average intercorrelation was .36.

The index of treatment responsibility in the Pilot Survey consisted of the following items. "Most people who don't get ahead shouldn't blame the system; they have only themselves to blame" (v8402), "If people work hard they almost always get what they want" (v8406), and "Any person who is willing to work hard has a good chance of succeeding" (v8204). The average inter-item correlation was .28.

The specific items used to measure information about poverty in the Pilot Study were variables 8512–8513, 8516, and 8519, which tap knowledge about the prevailing unemployment and inflation rates, and the partisan preference of poor people and blacks. The average inter-item correlation between these items was .24.

Racial Inequality

A five-point scale with end points of very poor and very good was used to record Reagan's performance concerning civil rights; evaluations of Jesse Jackson, civil rights leaders, and black people were made on a 100-point feeling thermometer; support for government civil rights programs was assessed using a seven-point scale; and finally, support for federal spending on civil rights programs was recorded on a three-point scale.

Crime

Support for the death penalty was assessed along a seven-point scale with end points of "strongly in favor" and "strongly opposed";

evaluations of Reagan's performance and the performance of judges followed the standard five-point scale ranging from "very good" to "very poor." The police were rated on the 100-point feeling thermometer; and finally, spending preferences on law enforcement were captured using the same three-point scale used previously.

Terrorism

Participants were asked to rate (on five-point scales) the degree to which President Reagan and the government of Israel had "affected the level of terrorism"; participants rated Colonel Qaddafi and the U.S. military along a 100-point feeling thermometer; spending preferences were indicated on a three-point scale; and finally, opinions concerning the use of force against governments that support terrorists were assessed with a seven-point scale featuring end points of "use military force" and "use diplomatic pressure."

Foreign Policy Opinions

In the framing study, the performance ratings were made with the standard five-point scales that ranged from "very good" to "very bad." The spending item followed past practice and consisted of "increase," "stay the same," and "decrease" categories. The Central American intervention, military retaliation against proterrorist governments, and U.S.–U.S.S.R. cooperation items were seven-point scales.

Turning to the various CBS News–New York Times surveys, the Contra-aid question, ratings of Colonel North, and perceptions of the significance of the issue were all taken from the 16 July survey, which included both the open-ended and closed-ended indicators of presidential responsibility. Assessments of the president's performance concerning Iran-Contra matters were taken from the December survey, which included only the closed-ended indicator of presidential responsibility ("Did the President know"). Finally, the question concerning the fairness of the Tower Commission Report was taken from the 28 February–1 March 1987 survey, which also included only the closed-ended indicator of presidential responsibility. The coefficients for attributions of presidential responsibility in table 7.7 thus reflect differing measures. In the case of the 16 July survey, the measure is the index of presidential responsibility; for the remaining surveys, the measure is simply whether the respondents said yes to the "did the President know" question. The exact wording of the various questions is given below.

Contra Aid. Do you approve or disapprove of the U.S. government giving military and other aid to the Contras who are fighting against the government of Nicaragua?

Colonel North. Here are some things people have said about Oliver North. Please tell me what you think.

Do you think Oliver North went too far with his actions?

Do you think he behaved as if he were above the law?

Do you think Oliver North is a national hero?

Do you think Oliver North is a real patriot?

An index was constructed by summing the yes or no responses.

Iran-Contra Salience. Is the Iran-Contra matter as serious for the country as Watergate was, or not?

Tower Commission. Do you think the Tower Commission Report was too hard on the Reagan administration, too easy on the Reagan administration, or was it fair?

Iran-Contra Performance. Do you approve of the way Ronald Reagan is handling the whole issue of Iranian arms sales and the Contras?

The exact wording of the questions used is given below.

Do you approve or disapprove of the way Ronald Reagan is handling foreign policy?

Is your opinion of Secretary of State George Schultz favorable, not favorable, undecided, or haven't you heard enough about him to have an opinion?

Do you think that Ronald Reagan has seen to it that most other countries respect the United States more today than they used to, or hasn't he?

Who do you trust to make the right decisions on foreign policy—Ronald Reagan, or Congress?

In making its decisions about terrorism, should the U.S. government be more concerned about the lives of the hostages, or more concerned about keeping its policy of never negotiating with terrorists?

Since 1979, the U.S. has observed the arms limits set by the SALT 2 agreement with the Soviet Union, even though the treaty was never approved by the Senate. Ronald Reagan has decided that the U.S. will no longer abide by these limits.

Do you approve or disapprove of Reagan's decision, or haven't you heard enough about it to have an opinion?

Do you approve or disapprove of the way Ronald Reagan is handling arms control negotiations with the Soviet Union?

Finally, the indicator of information varies from survey to survey. In most cases, "interest in the Iran-Contra hearings" was used as a substitute for information. In the 16 July survey, however, an information question was available—"Can you tell me what part of the world Nicaragua is in?

Partisan Differences in Attributions of Responsibility

In interpreting the results from the various correlational analyses reported in chapter 7, it is important to bear in mind that attributions of responsibility were far from surrogates for partisanship or political ideology. Causal and treatment attributions for poverty, unemployment, and racial inequality showed little variability with participants' political party affiliation or their political ideology. In general, self-reported liberals tended to favor societal over individualistic attributions, while conservatives revealed the opposite pattern. Similarly, by generally small margins, Republicans were more likely than Democrats to cite individualistic attributions.

Attributions of responsibility for crime and terrorism also differed only slightly depending upon participants' party affiliation and ideological identification. In general, conservatives and Republicans were less likely to offer societal attributions, while Democrats and liberals were more likely to do so. The clearest instance of this pattern was treatment responsibility for terrorism: 44 percent of liberals and 30 percent of Democrats cited societal treatment responsibility compared with 14 percent of conservatives and 9 percent of Republicans.

In the NES survey as well, attributions of responsibility for poverty were reasonably distinct from partisanship and ideology. The amount of variance in the indices of causal and treatment responsibility accounted for by partisanship and ideology was modest.

Since party identification and liberal-conservative orientation explained only small amounts of variation in attributions of causal and treatment responsibility for national issues, the contributions of the attribution measures to issue-specific opinions is distinct.

The solitary instance of significant partisan bias in attributions of responsibility was the Iran-Contra affair, where Democrats and Republicans differed significantly in their willingness to hold the president responsible. To adjust for this bias, the indicator of presidential responsibility in the "CBS News"–New York Times surveys (either the "did the president know" question or the sum of the "Did the President know" and "What did North lie about" questions) were regressed against four dummy variables corresponding to the two partisan and ideological groups. The residuals from this equation were then used to predict the various opinions in Tables 7.7 and 7.8.

General Opinions

Evaluations of the president's overall performance in the Suffolk County experiments were gauged with a single question: "How would you rate President Reagan's overall performance as President?" A battery of trait ratings were used to construct composite indices of competence and integrity. Respondents indicated that the degree to which the traits "knowledgeable," "hard-working," "experienced," and "intelligent" fit Reagan (using for each item a four-point scale that ranged from "extremely well" to "not well at all"). Responses to these items were highly correlated (across all the Suffolk County studies, the mean inter-item r was .68), and they were summed to form an index of competence. A similar procedure was followed with respect to the trust items—"fair," "honest," "compassionate," and "sympathetic." Here the average inter-item correlation (across all studies) was .48.

In the NES pilot survey, evaluations of Reagan's overall performance were gauged with a five-point scale that ranged from "very good" to "very poor" (V456 in the NES Codebook). Assessments of his competence and trustworthiness were measured with a battery of trait ratings. In the case of competence, respondents were asked to rate how well (using four response options that ranged from "extremely well" to "not well at all") the traits "knowledgeable," "provides strong leadership" and "intelligent" (V605, V609, V612 in the NES Codebook) described President Reagan. Responses were dichotomized and summed. The average intercorrelation (r) of the three individual items was .57. The trait terms making up the trustworthiness index included "fair," "compassionate," "decent," and "moral" (V602, V603, V606, and V614 in the NES Codebook). The average inter-item correlation for this set was .52.

In both "CBS News"–*New York Times* surveys, the overall performance question was the standard, "Do you approve or disapprove of the way Ronald Reagan is handling his job as President?" In the

November survey, an index of perceived presidential competence was constructed based on four questions.

1. Do you think Ronald Reagan has good judgment under pressure?
2. Do you think Ronald Reagan is a strong leader?
3. Do you think that Ronald Reagan understands the complicated problems a president has to deal with?
4. Do you have confidence in Ronald Reagan's ability to deal wisely with a difficult international crisis, or are you uneasy about his approach?

Responses (yes or no) to these questions were highly intercorrelated (the average inter-item r was .56), and they were added. The July survey included only a single question on competence: "Do you think that most of the time Ronald Reagan is in charge of what goes on in his administration, or do you think that most of the time other people are really running the government?"

The November survey included only one question on Reagan's personal integrity: "Do you think Ronald Reagan has more honesty and integrity than most people in public life?" The July survey did not include this or other questions on personal integrity.

The question tapping evaluations of Vice President Bush was worded as follows (the question was only available in the November survey): "Is your opinion of George Bush favorable, not favorable, undecided, or haven't you heard enough about him yet to have an opinion?"

Finally, the November survey included two questions measuring respondents' trust in the federal government.

1. How much of the time do you think you can trust the government in Washington to do what is right—just about always, most of the time, or only some of the time?
2. How much of the time do you think the administration in Washington tells the truth—all of the time, most of the time, or hardly ever?

Responses to the two questions were highly intercorrelated ($r = .47$) and were summed to form an index.

To address the issue of simultaneity (potential feedback from general evaluations of political leaders to attributions of responsibility for crime, terrorism, or racial inequality) in table 8.2, the evaluations of President Reagan were first purged of partisan and ideological influence and then used to predict the indices (both causal and treatment) of responsibility. This two-stage procedure was appropriate because the direct effects of partisanship and liberal-conservative orientation on attributions of responsibility for the issues in question were modest. The results of the two-stage analysis revealed no significant effects of the overall performance, competence, or integrity ratings on attributions, suggesting that the coefficents for these attributions in table 8.2 are not strongly contaminated with "rationalization" effects.

The indicator of presidential responsibility for the arms sale in the national surveys was similarly cleansed of partisan and ideological bias (table 8.4). Nonetheless, there can be no denying the presence of lingering "rationalization bias" in the indicator. That is, many individuals in these surveys may have encountered no specific information about President Reagan's awareness of the arms sale and related events. These individuals may have answered by simply projecting their general impression of the president. This is a fairly common bias in attitude research, whereby the specific traits or characteristics of some target person are "filled in" by the respondent's overall liking of the target person. Thus, the coefficients for the attribution indicator in table 8.4 can also be taken to indicate that people who held Reagan in high esteem were led to respond negatively to the "did the president know" question. Unfortunately, there is not much that can be done to unravel the flow of causal influence between attribution of responsibility for the arms sale and general approval of President Reagan in the national surveys, since both are subject to common antecedents such as partisanship and ideological orientation.

Indirect Effects

The percentage increases in an opinion's influence over general opinion's influence over general opinions were estimated by computing interaction terms between the issue-specific opinions and attributions and specifying the following equation:

General Evaluation $= b_0$Issue-Specific Opinion$_i$ $+$ b_1Index of Causal Responsibility$_i$ $+$ b_2 Index of Treatment Responsibility $+$ b_3(Issue-Specific Opinion$_i$ $\times$ Index of Causal Responsibility$_i$) $+$ b_4(Issue-Specific Opinion$_i$ $\times$ Index of Treatment Responsibility$_i$) $+$ b_5Party Affiliation $+$ b_6Political Ideology $+$ b_7Information $+$ b_8Socioeconomic Status $+$ e_i

In this equation the subscript i refers to the set of issues; the coefficients b_3 and b_4 represent the indirect effects of causal and treatment attributions, respectively. To the degree these coefficients are significant, assigning responsibility to societal (but not other) factors has the effect of strengthening the impact of issue-specific opinions on general evaluations. The percentage differences were computed from the coefficients b_3 and b_4.

It was not feasible to examine the indirect effects in a multivariate context because of the extremely high collinearities between the various interaction terms and between the specific issue opinions themselves.

Individual Differences

The analysis of individual characteristics was carried out in serial fashion, one characteristic being considered at a time. For the independent effects of the various dispositional characteristics to be estimated would require computation of several interaction terms (between the framing manipulation and particular dispositional characteristics). Because of the relatively small number of respondents in each study and the extreme collinearities between interaction terms and their components, a multivariate analysis was not feasible. For instance, the correlation between the framing × gender interaction term and gender is, by definition, very strong. It was therefore not feasible to evaluate the relative effects of particular audience characteristics.

Notes

Introduction

1. See Hearold 1986.

2. For a general review and summary of these arguments, see Ansolabehere, Behr, and Iyengar 1991.

3. See Weisman 1984; Weintraub 1985.

4. For a comprehensive review of agenda-setting research, see Rogers and Dearing 1988.

5. See Iyengar and Kinder 1987.

6. See Page and Shapiro 1987.

7. Neal Postman (1985), for example, has argued that television news is an inherently episodic medium.

8. See Altheide 1987; Paletz, Ayanian, and Fozzard 1982.

9. For evidence that network news coverage of the environment is heavily episodic, see Greenberg et al. 1989.

Chapter 1

1. For detailed and illuminating reviews of this vast literature, see Kinder 1983; Kinder and Sears 1985; Luskin 1987.

2. See, for example, Brady and Sniderman 1985; Hurwitz and Peffley 1987; Iyengar 1989.

3. For illustrative discussions of causal responsibility; see Fincham and Jaspars 1980; Shaver 1985; Kruglanski 1989. The concept of treatment responsibility is delineated in Brickman et al. 1982.

4. See Mayhew 1974; Fenno 1978; Denzau, Riker, and Shepsle 1985. For a discussion of some of the specific strategies politicians employ to claim or to evade responsibility, see Weaver 1986; McGraw 1990a, 1990b.

5. For evidence on the spontaneity of attribution, see Nisbett and Ross

1980; Weiner 1985a; Iyengar 1987. The illustrative experimental research concerning the attitudinal consequences of attribution is covered in Schneider, Hastorf, and Ellsworth 1979; Fiske and Taylor 1984; Brickman et al. 1982; Schachter 1964; Weiner 1985b. The nonlaboratory evidence is summarized in Bettman and Weitz 1983; Folkes 1984; Pettigrew 1979; Iyengar 1987.

6. For general reviews of this research concerning behavioral effects, see Lemkau, Bryant, and Brickman 1982; Langer and Rodin 1976; Rodin 1986; Lerner 1980.

7. See, for example, Langer 1975; Wortman 1976.

8. See Sniderman and Brody 1977; Lau and Sears 1981; Abramowitz, Lanoue, and Ramesh 1988.

9. Research dealing with the impact of economic conditions on political attitudes includes Key 1966; Fiorina 1981; Kiewiet 1983; Hibbs 1987; Hibbs, Rivers, and Vasilatos 1982; Abramowitz, Lanoue, and Ramesh 1988.

10. The evidence demonstrating situational specificity in behavior was first documented by Mischel 1968. This work, which directly challenged the "trait" conception of behavior, stimulated a widely ranging debate in social psychology over the relative influence of traits and situations as well as their interactive effects. For recent summaries, see Nisbett 1980; Kenrick and Funder 1988.

Chapter 2

1. The experimental evidence on framing can be found in Kahneman and Tversky 1982, 1984, 1987; Quattrone and Tversky 1988; Thaler 1987; Payne, Laughhunn, and Crum 1980; Slovic, Fischhoff, and Lichtenstein 1982.

2. Kahneman and Tversky 1984, p. 343.

3. Schelling 1984.

4. See McNeil et al. 1982.

5. Thaler 1980.

6. See Lane 1962. Lane's pioneering studies showed that ordinary people express uncertainty and even stress when describing their political views, and they often offer a hodge-podge of contradictory positions on related issues.

7. For an overview of the question-wording literature, see Schuman and Presser 1982; McClendon and O'Brien 1988. Although most of the research into framing of political opinions rests on survey evidence, there is a growing experimental literature concerning the effects of perceiving stimuli as either gains or losses on political judgments. See Quattrone and Tversky 1988; Ansolabehere, Iyengar, and Simon 1990.

8. See, for example, Sullivan, Piereson, and Marcus 1982.

9. See Smith 1987. There is also evidence that the degree of interconnectedness between opinion responses depends upon framing. For example, when affirmative action is described as an "unfair advantage" for blacks,

whites who support affirmative action also support civil rights. When affirmative action is described in terms of reverse discrimination against whites, however, the level of consistency between support for civil rights and affirmative action is reduced (see Kinder and Sanders 1986).

10. See Schuman and Presser 1982; Kahneman and Tversky 1984. For similar evidence that response instability is political surveys is not concentrated among the least educated or informed strata, see Achen 1975.

11. Kahneman and Tversky 1984, p. 343.

12. The presence or absence of talking heads is a critical diagnostic difference between the two news frames. Thematic coverage requires interviews with a variety of subject matter "experts" if it is to conform to norms of "objective" reporting. Episodic coverage typically excludes such expert sources.

13. These structural influences are discussed in Gans 1979; Roshco 1975; Arlen 1976; Weaver 1972; Ranney 1983.

14. The evidence is presented in Gitlin 1980; Gamson and Modigliani 1989.

15. This evidence, which is drawn from British television news, can be found in Halloran, Elliot, and Murdock 1970; Glasgow University Media Group 1976, 1980.

16. See Altheide 1987.

17. Altheide 1987, p. 300.

18. For the most recent evidence of horse-race coverage by television news, see Buchanan 1991; Hallin 1990.

19. These studies, which derive from the sociological tradition as developed by Bateson (1972) and Goffman (1974), do refer to media "framing"; however, they are distinct from the psychological literature on the effects of framing on choice problems and represent a quite different approach to the analysis of communications. The sociological studies tend to focus on the use of "story lines," symbols, and stereotypes in media presentations. These studies have found, for example, that news coverage of protests against the development of nuclear power typically depict participants as members of a radical counterculture by providing images of guitar-strumming, unkempt young people (see Gamson 1989). This literature thus defines news frames in terms of ideological or value perspectives (see Gitlin 1980; Cohen and Young 1981; Gamson and Modigliani 1989; Gamson and Lasch 1983; Gamson 1989). Although sociologists ascribe a very different meaning to the term "framing," it is interesting that their work and the research reported here conclude that television news has a significant proestablishment effect.

Chapter 3

1. For exceptions see Hovland 1959; Iyengar and Kinder 1987.

2. Detailed discussions of experimental research are provided in Carlsmith, Ellsworth, and Aronson 1976 and Campbell and Stanley 1966.

3. Of course, this is a probabilistic argument. It is possible that, despite random assignment, experimental conditions will differ in their composition. It is standard practice in experimental research to verify that random assignment achieves the desired effect. In none of the nine framing experiments did conditions differ significantly on any background factor.

4. The instructions stated, "Today television is the major source of information for Americans. This study is about how people evaluate, understand, and interpret television news stories. We are particularly interested in 'selective perception.' Do people's opinions about politics and government influence how they react to news? Do Republicans and Democrats really see the same news?"

5. The experimental procedure described here adhered to the American Psychological Association's guidelines on experimental research.

6. Despite their unwieldy nature, open-ended indicators are preferrable to fixed-choice, rating-scale indicators on several grounds. First, they are relatively unobtrusive and shield the researcher's intent from respondents. Second, since there is very little prior evidence from which to construct closed-ended items tapping attributions of causal and treatment responsibility, use of such indicators would have been risky. Finally, there is evidence in the attribution literature demonstrating that open-ended measures of responsibility achieve higher levels of predictive validity (see Russell, McAuley, and Jerico 1987).

7. When potential participants telephoned the Media Laboratory, they were screened according to various demographic factors, including age. Callers indicating that they were college students or younger than eighteen were turned away.

8. In each study participants were asked to record the emotions they felt while watching two of the videotaped stories (one of which was always the treatment story). The list of emotions included happiness, hope, fear, sadness, anger, and disgust. Their responses (yes or no) were than summed to form an index of affect. The first instance of significant differences in emotional arousal arose in the initial poverty experiment and was trivial because the two conditions that differed significantly with regard to affect elicited the identical pattern of causal and treatment attributions. The second instance of differential affect across conditions stemmed from the first terrorism experiment, and here the difference in affect was associated with differences in causal attributions (for further discussion of this result, see chapter 4).

9. For a detailed discussion of experimental demand, see Orne 1962.

Chapter 4
1. For similar findings based on a content analysis of newspapers, see Graber 1980. The extent to which the networks presented episodic reports on crime fluctuated, but episodic framing accounted for at least 75 percent of coverage of crime in every year.

2. See especially Paletz, Ayanian, and Fozzard 1982; Altheide 1987.

3. Altheide 1987, p. 174.

4. A similar breakdown of causal attributions for crime was obtained by Carroll et al. 1987 with a battery of closed-ended questions and a sample of "expert" attributors, namely, parole-board members and probation officers.

5. This aggregate-level similarity should not, however, be taken to imply that any given individual assigned responsibility for the two issues consistently. As the results in chapter 9 demonstrate, individual-level consistency in causal and treatment attributions for both issues was weak.

6. In every methodological respect except one this study was identical to all others. The exception was the use of a control group that watched no news report dealing with terrorism. This study was carried out in September 1985, shortly after the hijacking occurred.

7. See, for instance, Ross 1977; Jones 1979.

8. A plausible post hoc explanation for the high level of individualistic attributions for terrorism in the thematic U.S. Foreign Policy condition concerns affect. Because this report presented the hijacking as an expression of political opposition to the United States, and because President Reagan angrily condemned the terrorists, the story may have prompted a stronger "outgroup" stereotype (i.e., higher negative affect toward the hijackers) thus strengthening participants' inclination to cite terrorists' personal deficiencies as causal factors. The posttest questionnaire included a set of questions asking viewers whether the story on the hijacking had "made them feel" a variety of emotions, including "disgust," "anger," and "fear." These responses were summed to form a summary measure of negative affect. Participants in the U.S. Foreign Policy condition were significantly ($p < .05$) more aroused by the news report than were subjects in all remaining conditions. Moreover, across all conditions, the greater the arousal of negative affect, the greater the proportion of individual causes cited. In short, the presentation in the U.S. Foreign Policy condition unintentionally raised viewers' hostility toward the hijackers, thereby inducing individualistic attributions.

9. See, for example, Graber 1980.

10. Under these circumstances, there is an obvious risk of confounding the race of the perpetrator and the degree of "justifiability" of the criminal acts portrayed in the black and white episodic conditions. The Goetz case was included in the design because its high level of newsworthiness in the New York area made this incident highly representative of episodic news coverage of crime at the time of the study.

Chapter 5

1. See, for instance, McCloskey and Zaller 1984; Verba and Orren 1985; Bellah et al. 1985.

2. For evidence that Americans do hold poor people responsible for poverty, see Feagin 1975; Goodban 1981; Kluegel and Smith 1986; Feldman 1983;

Lewis and Schneider 1985; Verba and Orren 1985. For evidence of the same pattern in the case of unemployment, see Furnham 1982; Schlozman and Verba 1979. Finally, the tendency to attribute responsibility for racial inequality to black people is documented in Apostle et al. 1983; Sniderman and Hagen 1985.

3. Although accounting for a relatively small fraction of news coverage on racial inequality, the size of the affirmative action category increased from less than 5 percent during 1981–83 to 30 percent during 1984–86. Correspondingly, the number of discrimination stories and their relative share of news about racial inequality fell dramatically from 176 (76 percent of all coverage) during 1981–83 to 45 (33 percent) during 1984–86.

4. Episodic and thematic classification of unemployment and poverty stories was also analyzed on an annual basis. Thematic framing of unemployment predominated in every year, although episodic framing reached its highest levels (25 percent) during the recession years of 1982 and 1983. In the case of poverty, episodic framing accounted for a majority of the stories in each year except 1981, when thematic stories made up 55 percent of the total. This deviation from the general pattern was occasioned by an outpouring of thematic stories covering the congressional struggles over the Reagan administration's proposed cuts in social welfare programs.

5. In the case of both poverty and unemployment, the *spontaneity* of causal and treatment attributions was assessed by asking respondents, "When you hear or read about poverty/unemployment, what kinds of things do you think about? Please list as many thoughts as you have." Responses to this "thought-listing" question fell into four general categories: descriptions, explanations, expressions of affect, and prescriptions of treatments. For both issues, explanations and treatments made up more than 50 percent of all thoughts, suggesting that the causal and treatment responsibility are "natural" concepts. That is, causal and treatment attributions seem to be offered spontaneously when individuals think about political issues.

6. In addition to these societal and individual factors, a small percentage of the causal responses referred to what can best be described as "cultural" explanations. These consisted mainly of references to family characteristics (such as "broken homes" and "most people are born into poverty"). It was unclear whether the causal mechanism implicit in these responses was individual or societal in nature. These responses were therefore placed in a residual "other" category and excluded from further analysis.

7. Although economic explanations of unemployment overshadowed all others, no single facet of the economy or particular economic trend predominated; rather, respondents cited a wide variety of economic causes. Moreover, the responses in this category were often obscure, diffuse, and amorphous—i.e., "we're seeing a downturn in the economy," "businesses aren't hiring," etc. The frequency of economic causes is thus suggestive of

considerable ambiguity in attribution of causal responsibility for unemployment, a finding that mirrors earlier research. As Schlozman and Verba (1979, p. 194) report, even the unemployed (who might be expected to have a particular good understanding of responsibility) disagree among themselves: "some people blame everybody, others blame nobody, others are confused, and still others have individual theories."

8. The differences between poverty and unemployment are consistent with prior research that used very different (closed-ended) indicators of attribution (see Feagin 1975; Kluegel and Smith 1986; Goodban 1981; Furnham 1982; Feather and Davenport 1981). In the case of racial inequality, however, the heavily societal distribution of causal attributions found here deviates from earlier work based on closed-ended measures of explanations for inequality. Sniderman and Hagen (1985), for example, using both NES and local surveys, found that the public's predominant explanation of inequality was individualistic (see also Apostle et al. 1983). The closed-ended items used by these researchers, however, did not tap any of the societal categories uncovered here and referred instead to historical factors ("generations of slavery"), divine will, and conspiracy theory ("a small group of wealthy white people who act to keep blacks down"). These data are thus not readily comparable with the open-ended responses reported here.

9. See Brickman et al. 1982.

10. These were initially designed as separate conditions to assess the effects, if any, of the homeless person's race. In this particular study, however, the two conditions elicited a similar pattern of responses. For purposes of the analysis, they were treated as one condition.

11. See, for example, Walster 1966.

12. For evidence of such "wishful thinking" in attributions, see Lerner 1980; Shaver 1970.

13. See U.S. Congress 1985.

14. When the pooled thematic conditions were compared with the pooled episodic conditions, all four comparisons achieved statistical significance. When the news frame was thematic, societal causes and treatments outnumbered individualistic causes and treatments by a margin of more than two to one. In contrast, under conditions of episodic framing, the ratio of societal to individual causes and treatments approached equality.

Chapter 6

1. Since the seminal work by Neustadt (1960), a number of scholars have addressed the importance of popularity for the contemporary president. The list includes Cronin 1980; Kernell 1986; Light 1982; and Lowi 1985.

2. For further details on this classification of events, see Ostrom and Simon 1989.

3. Ibid.

4. Ross 1977; Jones 1979.

5. The five different surveys were conducted on 30 November 1986 (N = 687), 7–8 December 1986 (N = 1036), 28 February–1 March 1987 (N = 1174), 9 July 1987 (N = 658) and 16 July 1987 (N = 665).

6. This level of presidential responsibility is clearly higher than that recorded in the Suffolk County framing experiment and can be attributed to obvious differences in measurement. When respondents in the national survey were forced to choose between attributing responsibility to President Reagan or the "White House Staff," only 25 percent cited the president, a figure that is much closer to the breakdown of open-ended references to presidential responsibility in the Suffolk County framing experiment.

7. These two conditions also did not differ significantly in the relative frequency of references to President Reagan's competence or integrity as causal factors, although what differences did emerge were in the expected direction; that is, coverage of the president's misstatements, etc., did provoke a higher proportion of competence-oriented responses, while coverage of the president's credibility did elicit a slightly higher proportion of responses citing inadequate candor and trustworthiness.

8. Ostrom and Simon 1989, pp. 379–83.

Chapter 7

1. The relevant research is cited in footnotes 5–7 to chapter 1.

2. In the particular case of racial inequality, the percentage of causal and treatment attributions referring to affirmative action or preferential treatment were added to the percentage of individualistic attributions and subtracted from the percentage of societal attributions. Unemployment was excluded from this analysis since no framing effects were observed for this issue; however, the results of similar analyses with the unemployment data corroborated in all respects the results obtained for poverty and racial inequality.

3. See Kinder and Sears 1985.

4. Since most of the coefficients for these two predictors were nonsignificant, they were excluded from the tables that follow.

5. For instance, the equation predicting opinions toward the death penalty included a multiplicative term consisting of societal causal attribution and societal treatment attribution.

6. The equation predicting evaluations of the Israeli government's performance with respect to terrorism also included a dummy variable representing whether or not participants were Jewish.

Chapter 8

1. See Kinder 1986; Kinder and Sears 1985; Iyengar and Kinder 1987. See also appendix C.

2. Logically, it could follow equally well that respondents who attributed responsibility for poverty to individuals might also focus on their issue-specific opinions. Thus, they might give significant weight to a president's performance in restricting eligibility for "unnecessary" welfare programs; however, not a single such indirect effect was observed.

3. This evidence is described in Iyengar and Kinder 1987, chapter 9.

4. The trends in Reagan's popularity during his eight years in office are shown in Ostrom and Simon 1989.

5. Once again, caution is to be exercised in interpreting these results. As noted in chapter 7, attributions of responsibility for the arms sale and general impressions of President Reagan feed on each other.

6. See Lau 1982, 1985; Fiorina and Shepsle 1990; Born 1990; Ansolabehere 1988; Ansolabehere, Iyengar, and Simon 1990.

7. While there were nine significant interaction effects stemming from causal responsibility for poverty and racial inequality, there were only three associated with treatment responsibility.

8. Attributions of treatment responsibility for crime and terrorism induced a total of fifteen significant indirect effects, compared with a total of five for causal responsibility.

9. For evidence that people do entertain stereotypic beliefs concerning what presidents should and should not do, see Kinder et al. 1980.

10. See Lowi 1985, p. 173.

11. As several commentators have pointed out, the Reagan administration was particularly adept at this process of alternatively claiming and denying responsibility, giving rise to the apt label of the "Teflon presidency." For an analysis of strategies for evading political responsibility, see McGraw 1990b.

Chapter 9

1. See Kinder and Sears 1985.

2. For illustrative evidence of counter-argument as a mediator of media agenda-setting effects, see Iyengar and Kinder 1985.

3. See Roberts and Maccoby 1985; Bower 1985; Frank and Greenberg 1980.

4. Before pooling across the crime and terrorism conditions, the effects of the dispositional characteristics were investigated for each issue separately. No inconsistent relationships were detected. The same procedure (with the same outcome) was followed prior to pooling the two poverty experiments.

5. For the statistically inclined reader, the entries are mean residuals obtained by regressing the responsibility scores against the framing manipulation and subtracting respondents' actual responsibility score from the predicted score. Negative entries indicate that the group's actual responsibility score was underpredicted by the manipulation, i.e., that group members became less societal in their attributions under thematic framing than the

rest of the sample. Conversely, positive scores indicate that group members became more societal than might be expected, given the overall effects of thematic framing.

Audience characteristics that were found to have no noticeable effect on the extent of framing (here defined as any difference not achieving statistical significance at the .15 level according to a two-tailed t-test) were excluded from the table.

6. Republicans were not particularly resistant to political framing, because virtually *all* Republicans in the study, regardless of the experimental condition to which they were assigned, shied away from attributing responsibility to President Reagan.

7. The first test is essentially an aggregate indicator of spillover, while the second provides an individual-level indicator.

8. The impact of framing on inter-issue consistency was examined by specifying the following equation:

$$\text{Attribution}_{crime} = b_1(\text{Attribution}_{terrorism}) + b_2(\text{Framing}_{terrorism}) + b_3(\text{Attribution}_{terrorism} \times \text{Framing}_{terrorism})$$

The coefficient b_3 gauges the degree to which framing of terrorism affects the interdependence of crime and terrorism attributions. In the crime-terrorism study, three of the four relevant interaction coefficients were significant at the .15 level or better. In the case of the poverty-unemployment study, neither of the interaction terms proved significant.

9. In fact, the effects of crime and terrorism coverage on viewers' attributions of responsibility for racial inequality were nonexistent. Conversely, the subject matter news frames for racial inequality (black poverty, affirmative action, and discrimination) had no discernible impact on attributions for terrorism. Framing racial inequality in terms of discrimination, however, did serve to increase ($p < .10$) the level of societal treatment attributions for crime.

Conclusion

1. For evidence concerning levels of political knowledge, see Kinder and Sears 1985.

2. For further discussion of domain specificity in political thinking, see Iyengar 1990.

3. See Converse 1964; Lane 1962.

4. Converse 1964, p. 247.

5. An identical experimental design to that used in the framing studies produced significant delayed effects on participants' responses. In this study, participants were asked (one week following their exposure to the news), "What do you think are the three most important problems facing the country at present?" Their responses tended to reflect the content of the news

coverage, thus suggesting persistence of media agenda-setting effects for at least one week. See Iyengar and Kinder 1987 for additional details on this and related experiments.

6. For evidence that values shape political opinions, see Feldman 1983; Sniderman and Brody 1977. That significant racial framing effects occur in the areas of crime and poverty is itself evidence that widely shared cultural norms and stereotypes are important prompts when individuals attribute responsibility for political issues.

7. See Wyer and Srull 1986. Although Wyer and Srull do not themselves make this point, it is likely that information considered particularly valuable or important (e.g., a candidate's stand on the budget deficit for a staunchly conservative voter) is also accorded preferential location in long-term storage, thus accounting for "chronic" or persistent accessibility effects.

For alternative accounts of long-term memory, information retrieval, and the accessibility bias, see Anderson 1983; Collins and Loftus 1975; Craik and Lockhart 1972; Rumelhart and Ortony 1977.

8. Slovic, Fischhoff, and Lichtenstein 1980, p. 127. For reviews of the various strands of decision-making and judgment research, see Einhorn and Hogarth 1981; Abelson and Levi 1985; Kahneman, Slovic, and Tversky 1982.

9. For research summarizing this evidence see Taylor and Fiske 1979; Wyer and Srull 1984; Higgins, Bargh, and Lombardi 1985; Sherman and Corty 1984; Bargh 1985; Taylor 1982.

10. See Slovic, Fischhoff, and Lichtenstein 1980.

11. For a general review of these studies, see Wyer and Hartwick 1980; Higgins and King 1981.

12. For a review of this work, see Fazio 1990; Fazio and Williams 1986. Parallel accessibility effects have been detected in studies of survey responses.

13. The most comprehensive review of the huge agenda-setting literature is to be found in Rogers and Dearing 1988.

14. This evidence is summarized in Iyengar and Kinder 1987, chapter 7.

15. For details on these studies, see Iyengar and Kinder 1987, chapter 8.

16. See Krosnick and Kinder 1990.

17. For a comprehensive analysis of the prevalence of horse-race coverage in television and newspaper accounts of the 1988 presidential campaign, see Buchanan 1991. While the tide of horse-race coverage naturally tends to boost front-runners, there is also a bonus for candidates who exceed journalistic expectations, that is, candidates who perform better than expected in the race. Gary Hart, for instance, ran third in the 1984 New Hampshire Democratic primary; since at that time he was quite obscure, this outcome itself induced a tremendous outpouring of media attention.

18. Bartels 1988, p. 42.

19. Evidence on this score is provided in Popkin, forthcoming.

20. See Bartels 1988, chapter 6; Bartels 1985; Brady 1984.

21. See Bishop, Oldendick and Tuchfarber 1982.

22. For general discussions of the importance of accessibility effects in survey research, see Zaller and Feldman 1988; Bishop, Oldendick, and Tuchfarber 1982. Tourangeau, Rasinski, and D'Andrade 1989 provide direct evidence that the accessibility of particular subjects reduces the amount of time in which respondents answer survey questions about these subjects.

23. For reviews of this and related studies, see Kinder and Sears 1985; Iyengar and Kinder 1987.

24. The Bush campaign aired a television commercial showing Governor Dukakis riding in an army tank with the announcer describing Bush's superior experience in the area of defense.

25. See Petrocik 1990. For discussion of the influence of political candidates over the media agenda, see Arterton 1978; Grossman and Kumar 1981; Hart 1987; Mickelson 1989.

26. For detailed analyses of the importance of these factors in influencing the content of the news, see Epstein 1973; Gans 1979; Tuchman 1978; Westin 1982.

27. For some evidence concerning the correspondence between network news coverage of the economy and economic realities, see Behr and Iyengar 1985; Harrington 1989.

28. See Lane 1962; Converse 1964; Kinder and Sears 1985.

29. The model is outined by Gitlin 1980; Donald and Hall 1986; Seidel 1975; Edelman 1977. For illustrative evidence, see Gitlin 1980; Jensen 1987; Cohen and Young 1981; Fishman 1980; Glasgow University Media Group 1980.

30. See, for example, Nisbett and Ross 1980.

31. Similar results are reported by Iyengar and Kinder (1987) who found that case-study coverage of unemployment and pollution dampened, rather than fanned, viewers' concern for these issues.

32. See Roshco 1975; Gans 1972.

33. Bagdikian 1985, p. 103.

34. See Gamson and Modigliani 1986.

35. See, for instance, Compaine 1985; Bagdikian 1983; Bennett 1990.

36. Postman 1985, p. 110.

37. For evidence that the American press typically adopts a "deferential" posture vis-à-vis political elites, see Bennett 1990; Boylan 1986.

38. For discussions of "retrospective" voting in American elections and its influence on policy makers, see Key 1964; Fiorina 1981; Brody and Page 1972; Mayhew 1974.

39. Cited in *Time*, 23 October 1989.

40. "Letter from Washington," *The New Yorker,* 30 October 1989, p. 106.

41. Evidence on the shrinking size of the sound bite is presented in Hallin 1990.

42. See Germond and Witcover 1989.

43. Germond and Witcover 1989, p. 459.

References

Abelson, Robert P., and Ariel Levi. 1985. Decision making. In Gardner Lindzey and Elliot Aronson (eds.), *The handbook of social psychology*, vol. 1. New York: Random House.

Abramowitz, Alan I., David J. Lanoue, and Subha Ramesh. 1988. Economic conditions, causal attributions, and political evaluations in the 1984 presidential election. *Journal of Politics* 50: 848–63.

Achen, Christopher H. 1975. Mass political attitudes and the survey response. *American Political Science Review* 69: 1218–31.

Altheide, David L. 1987. Format and symbol in television coverage of terrorism in the United States and Great Britain. *International Studies Quarterly* 31: 161–76.

Anderson, John R. 1983. *The architecture of cognition*. Cambridge: Harvard Univ. Press.

Ansolabehere, Stephen. 1988. Rational choice and the puzzle of negative voting: A random utilities model of the vote. Paper presented at the Annual Meeting of the Midwestern Political Science Association.

Ansolabehere, Stephen, Shanto Iyengar, and Adam Simon. 1990. Good news, bad news, and economic voting. Paper presented at the Annual Meeting of the American Political Science Association.

Ansolabehere, Stephen, Roy L. Behr, and Shanto Iyengar. 1991. Mass media and elections: An overview. *American Politics Quarterly* 19: 109–39.

Apostle, Richard A., Charles Y. Glock, Thomas Piazza, and Marijean Suelzle. 1983. *The anatomy of racial attitudes*. Berkeley and Los Angeles: Univ. of California Press.

Arlen, Michael J. 1976. *The view from highway 1: Essays on television*. New York: Farrar, Strauss & Giroux.

Arterton, Christopher F. 1978. The media politics of presidential campaigns.

In James D. Barber (ed.), *Race for the presidency: The media and the nominating process.* Englewood Cliffs, N.J.: Prentice-Hall.

Bagdikian, Ben H. 1983. *The media monopoly.* Boston: Beacon Press.

———. 1985. The U.S. media: Supermarket or assembly line? *Journal of Communication* 35: 97–109.

Bargh, John A. 1985. Automatic and conscious processing of social information. In Robert S. Wyer, Jr., and Thomas K. Srull (eds.), *Handbook of social cognition,* vol. 3. Hillsdale, N.J.: Lawrence Erlbaum Associates.

Bartels, Larry M. 1985. Expectations and preferences in presidential nominating campaigns. *American Political Science Review* 79: 804–15.

———. 1988. *Presidential primaries and the dynamics of public choice.* Princeton, N.J.: Princeton Univ. Press.

Bateson, Gregory. 1972. *Steps to an ecology of mind: Collected essays in anthropology, psychiatry, evolution, and epistemology.* San Francisco: Chandler Publishing Company.

Behr, Roy L., and Shanto Iyengar. 1985. Television news, real-world cues, and changes in the public agenda. *The Public Opinion Quarterly* 49: 38–57.

Bellah, Robert N., Richard Madsen, William M. Sullivan, Ann Swidler, and Steven M. Tipton. 1985. *Habits of the heart: Individualism and commitment in American life.* Berkeley and Los Angeles: Univ. of California Press.

Bennett, W. Lance. 1990. Toward a theory of press-state relations in the United States. *Journal of Communication* 40: 103–25.

Bettman, James R., and Barton A. Weitz. 1983. Attributions in the board room: Causal reasoning in corporate annual reports. *Administrative Science Quarterly* 28: 165–83.

Bishop, George F., Robert W. Oldendick, and Alfred J. Tuchfarber. 1982. Political information processing: Question order and context effects. *Political Behavior* 4: 177–200.

Born, Richard. 1990. Surge and decline, negative voting, and the midterm loss phenomenon: A simultaneous choice analysis. *American Journal of Political Science* 34: 615–45.

Bower, Robert T. 1985. *The changing television audience in America.* New York: Columbia Univ. Press.

Boylan, James. 1986. Declarations of independence. *Columbia Journalism Review,* Nov./Dec., 29-46.

Brady, Henry E. 1984. Chances, utilities, and voting in presidential primaries. Paper delivered at the Annual Meeting of the Public Choice Society, Phoenix, Ariz.

Brady, Henry E., and Paul M. Sniderman. 1985. Attitude attribution: A group basis for political reasoning. *American Political Science Review* 79: 1061–78.

References

Brickman, Phillip, James Karuza, Jr., Dan Coates, Ellen Cohn, and Louise Kidder. 1982. Models of helping and coping. *American Psychologist* 37: 368–84.

Brody, Richard A., and Benjamin I. Page. 1972. The assessment of policy voting. *American Political Science Review* 66: 450–58.

Buchanan, Bruce. 1991. *Electing a president: The Markle commission report on campaign '88.* Austin: Univ. of Texas Press, forthcoming.

Campbell, Donald T., and Julian C. Stanley. 1966. *Experimental and quasi-experimental designs for research.* Chicago: Rand McNally & Co.

Carlsmith, J. Merrill, Phoebe C. Ellsworth, and Elliot Aronson. 1976. *Methods of research in social psychology.* Reading, Mass.: Addison-Wesley.

Carroll, John S., William T. Perkowitz, Arthur J. Lurigio, and Frances M. Weaver. 1987. Sentencing goals, causal attributions, ideology, and personality. *Journal of Personality and Social Psychology* 52: 107–18.

Cohen, Stanley, and Jock Young. 1981. *The manufacture of news: Social problems, deviance, and the mass media.* London: Constable.

Collins, A. M., and Elizabeth F. Loftus. 1975. A spreading-activation theory of semantic processing. *Psychological Review* 82: 407–28.

Compaine, Benjamin M. 1985. The expanding base of media competition. *Journal of Communication* 35: 81–96.

Converse, Phillip E. 1964. The nature of belief systems in mass publics. In David Apter (ed.), *Ideology and discontent.* New York: The Free Press.

Craik, Fergus I., and R. S. Lockhart. 1972. Levels of processing: A framework for memory research. *Journal of Verbal Learning and Verbal Behavior* 11: 671–84.

Cronin, Thomas E. 1980. *The state of the presidency.* Boston: Little, Brown & Co.

Denzau, Arthur, William Riker, and Kenneth Shepsle. 1985. Farquharson and Fenno: Sophisticated voting and home style. *American Political Science Review* 79: 1117–34.

Donald, James, and Stuart Hall. 1986. *Politics and ideology: A Reader.* Philadelphia: Open Univ. Press.

Drew, Elizabeth. 1989. Letter from Washington. *The New Yorker,* 30 Oct.

Edelman, Murray J. 1977. *Political language: Words that succeed and policies that fail.* New York: Academic Press.

Einhorn, Hillel J., and Robin M. Hogarth. 1981. Behavioral decision theory. *Annual Review of Psychology,* vol. 32. Palo Alto, Calif.: Annual Review, Inc.

Epstein, Edward J. 1973. *News from nowhere.* New York: Random House.

Fazio, Russell H. 1990. Multiple processes by which attitudes guide behavior: The Mode model as an integrative framework. In Mark P. Zanna (ed.), *Advances in experimental social psychology,* vol. 23. New York: Academic Press.

Fazio, Russell H., and C. J. Williams. 1986. Attitude accessibility as a moderator of the attitude-perception and attitude-behavior relations: An investigation of the 1984 presidential election. *Journal of Personality and Social Psychology* 51: 505–14.

Feagin, Joseph. 1975. *Subordinating the poor: Welfare and American beliefs.* Englewood Cliffs, N.J.: Prentice-Hall.

Feather, Norman T., and Philip Davenport. 1981. Unemployment and depressive affect: A motivational and attributional analysis. *Journal of Personality and Social Psychology* 41: 422–36.

Feldman, Stanley. 1983. Economic individualism and American public opinion. *American Politics Quarterly* 11: 3–29.

Fenno, Richard F., Jr. 1978. *Home style: House members in their districts.* Boston: Little, Brown & Co.

Fincham, Frank D., and Jos M. Jaspars. 1980. Attribution of responsibility: From man the scientist to man as lawyer. In Leonard Berkowitz (ed.), *Advances in experimental social psychology* vol. 16. New York: Academic Press.

Fiorina, Morris J. 1981. *Retrospective voting in American national elections.* New Haven, Conn.: Yale Univ. Press.

Fiorina, Morris J., and Kenneth A. Shepsle. 1990. A positive theory of negative voting. In John Ferejohn and James Kuklinski (eds.), *Information and democratic processes.* Urbana: Univ. of Illinois Press.

Fishman, Mark. 1980. *Manufacturing the news.* Austin: Univ. of Texas Press.

Fiske, Susan T., and Shelley E. Taylor. 1984. *Social cognition.* New York: Random House.

Folkes, Valerie S. 1984. Consumer reactions to product failure: An attributional approach. *Journal of Consumer Research* 10: 398–409.

Frank, Ronald E., and Marshall G. Greenberg. 1980. *The public's use of television.* Beverly Hills: Sage Publications.

Furnham, Adrian. 1982. Explanations for unemployment in Britain. *European Journal of Social Psychology* 12: 335–52.

Furnham, Adrian, and Alan Lewis. 1986. *The economic mind.* Brighton: Wheatsheaf.

Gamson, William A. 1989. News as framing. *American Behavioral Scientist* 33: 157–61.

Gamson, William A., and Kathryn E. Lasch. 1983. The political culture of social welfare policy. In Shimon E. Sprio and Ephraim Yuchtman-Yaar (eds.), *Evaluating the welfare state: Social and political perspectives.* New York: Academic Press.

Gamson, William A., and Andre Modigliani. 1989. Media discourse and public opinion on nuclear power. *American Journal of Sociology* 95: 1–37.

Gans, Herbert. 1972. The famine in American mass communications research: Comments on Hirsch, Tuchman, and Gecas. *American Journal of Sociology* 77: 697–705.

References

———. 1979. *Deciding what's news*. New York: Pantheon Books.

Germond, Jack W., and Jules Witcover. 1989. *Whose broad stripes and bright stars? The trivial pursuit of the presidency, 1988*. New York: Warner Books.

Gitlin, Todd. 1980. *The whole world is watching*. Berkeley and Los Angeles: Univ. of California Press.

Glasgow University Media Group. 1976. *Bad news*. London: Routledge & Kegan Paul.

———. 1980. *More bad news*. London: Routledge & Kegan Paul.

Goffman, Erving. 1974. *Frame analysis: An essay on the organization of experience*. Cambridge: Harvard Univ. Press.

Goodban, Nancy. 1981. *Attributions about poverty*. Ph.D. diss., Harvard Univ.

Graber, Doris A. 1980. *Crime news and the public*. New York: Praeger.

Greenberg, Michael R., David B. Sechsman, Peter M. Sandman, and Kandice L. Salomone. 1989. Risk, drama, and geography in coverage of environmental risk by network television. *Journalism Quarterly* 66: 267–76.

Grossman, Michael B., and Martha J. Kumar. 1981. *Portraying the president: The White House and the news media*. Baltimore: Univ. of Maryland Press.

Hallin, Daniel C. 1990. Sound bite news. In Gary Orren (ed.), *Blurring the lines*. New York: The Free Press.

Halloran, James D., Philip Elliot, and Graham Murdock. 1970. *Demonstrations and communication: A case study*. Harmondsworth: Penguin Books.

Harrington, David E. 1989. Economic news on television. *Public Opinion Quarterly* 53: 17–40.

Hart, Roderick P. 1987. *The sound of leadership*. Chicago: Univ. of Chicago Press.

Hearold, Susan. 1986. A synthesis of 1,043 effects of television on social behavior. In George Comstock (ed.), *Public communication and behavior*, vol. 1. New York: Academic Press.

Hibbs, Douglas A., Jr. 1987. *The American political economy: Macroeconomics and electoral politics in the United States*. Cambridge: Harvard Univ. Press.

Hibbs, Douglas, A., Jr., Douglas Rivers, and Nicholas Vasilatos. 1982. On the demand for economic outcomes: Macroeconomic performance and mass political support in the United States, Great Britain, and Germany. *Journal of Politics* 44: 426–62.

Higgins, E. Tory, and Gillian King. 1981. Category accessibility and information processing: Consequences of individual and contextual variability. In Nancy Cantor and John Kihlstrom (eds.), *Personality, cognition, and social interaction*. Hillsdale, N.J.: Lawrence Erlbaum Associates.

Higgins, E. Tory, John A. Bargh, and W. Lombardi. 1985. Nature of priming effects on categorization. *Journal of Experimental Psychology: Learning, Memory, and Cognition* 11: 59–69.

Hovland, Carl I. 1959. Reconciling conflicting results derived from experimental and survey studies of attitude change. *American Psychologist* 14: 8–17.

Hurwitz, Jon, and Mark Peffley. 1987. How are foreign policy attitudes structured? A hierarchical model. *American Political Science Review* 81: 1099–1120.

Iyengar, Shanto. 1987. Television news and citizens' explanations of national issues. *American Political Science Review* 81: 815–32.

———. 1989. How citizens think about political issues: A matter of responsibility. *American Journal of Political Science* 33: 878–900.

———. 1990. Shortcuts to political knowledge: Selective attention and the accessibility bias. In John Ferejohn and James Kuklinski (eds.), *Information and the democratic process.* Urbana: Univ. of Illinois Press.

Iyengar, Shanto, and Donald R. Kinder. 1985. Psychological accounts of agenda-setting. In Richard Perloff and Sidney Kraus (eds.), *Mass media and political thought.* Beverly Hills: Sage Publications.

———. 1987. *News that matters.* Chicago: Univ. of Chicago Press.

Jensen, Klaus. 1987. News as ideology: Economic statistics and political ritual in television network news. *Journal of Communication* 37: 8–27.

Jones, Edward E. 1979. The rocky road from acts to dispositions. *American Psychologist* 34: 107–17.

Kahneman, Daniel, and Amos Tversky. 1982. The psychology of preferences. *Science* 246: 136–42.

———. 1984. Choices, values, and frames. *American Psychologist* 39: 341–50.

———. 1987. Rational choice and the framing of decisions. In Hillel J. Einhorn and Robin M. Hogarth (eds.), *Rational choice: The contrast between economics and psychology.* Chicago: Univ. of Chicago Press.

Kahneman, Daniel, Paul Slovic, and Amos Tversky (eds.). 1982. *Judgment under uncertainty: Heuristics and biases.* London: Cambridge Univ. Press.

Kenrick, Douglas T., and David C. Funder. 1988. Profiting from controversy: Lessons from the person-situation debate. *American Psychologist* 43: 23–34.

Kernell, Samuel. 1986. *Going public.* Washington: Congressional Quarterly Press.

Key, V. O., Jr. 1964. *Politics, parties, and pressure groups.* New York: Thomas Young Crowell Co.

———. 1966. *The responsible electorate.* Cambridge: Harvard Univ. Press.

Kiewiet, D. Roderick 1983. *Macroeconomics and micropolitics: The electoral effects of economic issues.* Chicago: Univ. of Chicago Press.

References

Kinder, Donald R. 1983. Diversity and complexity in American public opinion. In Ada W. Finifter (ed.), *Political science: The state of the discipline.* Washington, D.C.: American Political Science Association.

————. 1986. Presidential character revisited. In Richard R. Lau and David O. Sears (eds.), *Political cognition: The nineteenth annual Carnegie symposium on cognition.* Hillsdale, N.J.: Lawrence Erlbaum Associates.

Kinder, Donald R., and D. Roderick Kiewiet. 1979. Economic discontent and political behavior: The role of personal grievances and collective judgments in congressional voting. *American Journal of Political Science* 23: 495–527.

Kinder, Donald R., Mark D. Peters, Robert P. Abelson, and Susan T. Fiske. 1980. Presidential prototypes. *Political Behavior* 2: 315–37.

Kinder, Donald R., and David O. Sears. 1985. Public opinion and political behavior. In Gardner Lindzey and Elliot Aronson (eds.), *Handbook of social psychology,* vol. 2. New York: Random House.

Kinder, Donald R., and Lori Sanders. 1986. Revitalizing the measurement of white Americans' racial attitudes: A report to the NES Board of Overseers. Univ. of Michigan. Mimeo.

Kluegel, James, and Elliot R. Smith. 1986. *Beliefs about inequality.* New York: Aldine de Gruyter.

Koenig, Louis W. 1986. *The chief executive.* New York: Harcourt Brace Jovanovich.

Krosnick, Jon A., and Donald R. Kinder. 1990. Altering the foundations of popular support for the president through priming. *American Political Science Review* 84: 497–512.

Kruglanski, Arie W. 1989. *Lay epistemics and human knowledge: Cognitive and motivational biases.* New York: Plenum Press.

Lane, Robert E. 1962. *Political ideology: Why the common man believes what he does.* New York: The Free Press.

Langer, Ellen J. 1975. The illusion of control. *Journal of Personality and Social Psychology* 32: 311–28.

Langer, Ellen J., and Judith Rodin. 1976. The effects of choice and enhanced personal responsibility for the aged: A field experiment in an institutional setting. *Journal of Personality and Social Psychology* 34: 191–98.

Lau, Richard R. 1982. Negativity in political perception. *Political Behavior* 4: 353–78.

————. 1985. Two explanations for negativity effects in political behavior. *American Journal of Political Science* 29: 119–38.

Lau, Richard R., and David O. Sears. 1981. Cognitive links between economic grievances and political responses. *Political Behavior* 3: 279–302.

Lemkau, James, F. B. Bryant, and Phillip Brickman. 1982. Client commitment in the helping relationship. In T. A. Mills (ed.), *Basic processes in helping relationships.* New York: Aldine de Gruyter.

Lerner, Melvin. 1980. *The belief in a just world.* New York: Plenum Press.

Lewis, Irving, and William Schneider. 1985. Hard times: The public on poverty. *Public Opinion* 9: 2–7.

Light, Paul. 1982. *The president's agenda.* Baltimore, Md.: Johns Hopkins Univ. Press.

Lowi, Theodore J. 1985. *The personal president: Power invested, promise unfulfilled.* Ithaca, N.Y.: Cornell Univ. Press.

Luskin, Robert C. 1987. Measuring politial sophistication. *American Journal of Political Science* 31: 856–99.

McClendon, McKee J., and David J. O'Brien. 1988. Question-order effects on subjective well-being. *Public Opinion Quarterly* 52: 351–64.

McCloskey, Herbert, and John Zaller. 1984. *The American ethos: Public attitudes toward capitalism and democracy.* Cambridge: Harvard Univ. Press.

McGraw, Kathleen M. 1990a. Avoiding blame: An experimental study of political excuses and justifications. *British Journal of Political Science* 20: 119–42.

———. 1990b. Managing blame: An experimental investigation of the effectiveness of political accounts. Department of Political Science, State Univ. of New York at Stony Brook. Mimeo.

McNeil, Barbara, Steven Parker, Harold Sox, Jr., and Amos Tversky. 1982. On the elicitation of preferences for alternative therapies. *New England Journal of Medicine* 306: 1259–62.

Mayhew, David. 1974. *The electoral connection.* New Haven, Conn.: Yale Univ. Press.

Mickelson, Sig. 1989. *From whistle stop to sound bite: Four decades of politics and television.* New York: Praeger.

Mischel, Walter. 1968. *Personality and assessment.* New York: John Wiley & Sons.

National Election Studies. 1986. *1985 pilot study codebook.* Ann Arbor, Mich.: Center for Political Studies.

Neustadt, Richard. 1960. *Presidential power.* New York: John Wiley, & Sons.

Nisbett, Richard E. 1980. The trait construct in lay and professional psychology. In Leon Festinger (ed.), *Retrospections on social psychology.* New York: Oxford Univ. Press.

Nisbett, Richard E., and Lee Ross. 1980. *Human inference: Strategies and shortcomings of social judgment.* Englewood Cliffs, N.J.: Prentice-Hall.

Orne, Martin T. 1962. On the social psychology of the psychological experiment. *American Psychologist* 17: 776–83.

Ostrom, Charles W., Jr., and Dennis M. Simon. 1989. The man in the Teflon suit? *Public Opinion Quarterly* 53: 353–87.

Page, Benjamin I., and Robert Y. Shapiro. 1987. What moves public opinion? *American Political Science Review* 81: 23–43.

References

Paletz, David, J. Ayanian, and P. Fozzard. 1982. Terrorism on television news: The IRA, the FALN, and the Red Brigades. In William Adams (ed.), *Television coverage of international affairs*. Norwood, N.J.: Ablex.

Payne, John W., D. Laughhunn, and R. Crum. 1980. Translation of gambles and aspiration-level effects in risky-choice behavior. *Management Science* 26: 1039–60.

Petrocik, John R. 1990. The theory of issue ownership: Issues, agendas, and electoral coalitions in the 1988 election. Department of Political Science, Univ. of California, Los Angeles. Mimeo.

Pettigrew, Thomas. 1979. The ultimate attribution error: Extending Allport's analysis of prejudice. *Personality and Social Psychology Bulletin* 5: 461–76.

Popkin, Samuel L. 1991. *The reasoning voter*. Chicago: Univ. of Chicago Press, forthcoming.

Postman, Neal. 1985. *Amusing ourselves to death*. New York: Viking.

Quattrone, George A., and Amos Tversky. 1988. Contrasting rational and psychological analyses of political choice. *American Political Science Review* 82: 719–36.

Ranney, Austin. 1983. *Channels of power*. New York: Basic Books.

Roberts, Donald F., and Nathan Maccoby. 1985. Effects of mass communication. In Gardner Lindzey and Elliot Aronson (eds.), *Handbook of social psychology*, vol. 2. New York: Random House.

Rodin, Judith. 1986. Aging and health: Effects of the sense of control. *Science* 233: 1271–76.

Rogers, Everett M., and James W. Dearing. 1988. Agenda-setting research: Where has it been and where is it going? In James A. Anderson (ed.), *Communication yearbook*, vol. 11. Beverley Hills: Sage Publications.

Roshco, Bernard. 1975. *Newsmaking*. Chicago: Univ. of Chicago Press.

Ross, Lee. 1977. The intuitive psychologist and his shortcomings. In Leonard Berkowitz (ed.), *Advances in experimental social psychology*, vol. 10. New York: Academic press.

Rumelhart, David E., and Antony Ortony. 1977. The representation of knowledge in memory. In Richard C. Anderson, Rand J. Spiro, and William E. Montague (eds.), *Schooling and the acquisition of knowledge*. Hillsdale, N.J.: Lawrence Erlbaum Associates.

Russell, Daniel, Edward McAuley, and Valerie Jerico. 1987. Measuring causal attributions for success and failure: A comparison of methodologies for assessing causal dimensions. *Journal of Personality and Social Psychology* 52: 1248–57.

Schachter, Stanley. 1964. The interaction of cognitive and physiological components of emotional state. In Leonard Berkowitz (ed.), *Advances in experimental social psychology*, vol. 1. New York: Academic Press.

Schelling, Thomas C. 1984. *Choice and consequence: Perspectives of an errant economist*. Cambridge: Harvard Univ. Press.

Schlozman, Kay, and Sidney Verba. 1979. *Insult to injury: Unemployment, class, and political response.* Cambridge: Harvard Univ. Press.

Schneider, David. J., Albert H. Hastorf, and Phoebe C. Ellsworth. 1979. *Person perception.* Reading, Mass.: Addison-Wesley.

Schuman, Howard, and Stanley Presser. 1982. *Questions and answers in attitude surveys: Experiments on question form, wording, and context.* New York: Academic Press.

Seidel, G. 1975. Ambiguity in political discourse. In Maurice Bloch (ed.), *Political language and oratory in traditional society.* New York: Academic Press.

Shaver, Kelley G. 1970. Defensive attribution: Effects of severity and relevance on the responsibility assigned for an accident. *Journal of Personality and Social Psychology* 14: 101–13.

———. 1985. *The attribution of blame: Causality, responsibility, and blameworthiness.* New York: Springer-Verlag.

Sherman, Steven J., and Eric Corty. 1984. Cognitive heuristics. In Robert S. Wyer, Jr. and Thomas K. Srull (eds.), *Handbook of social cognition,* vol. 1. Hillsdale, N.J.: Lawrence Erlbaum Associates.

Slovic, Paul, Baruch Fischhoff, and Sarah Lichtenstein. 1980. Knowing what you want: Measuring labile values. In Thomas S. Wallsten (ed.), *Cognitive processes in choice and decision behavior.* Hillsdale, N.J.: Lawrence Erlbaum Associates.

———. 1982. Response mode, framing, and information-processing effects in risk assessment. In Robin M. Hogarth (ed.), *New directions for methodology of social and behavioral science: Question framing and response consistency.* San Francisco: Jossey-Bass.

Smith, Tom. 1987. That which we call welfare by any other name would smell sweeter: An analysis of the impact of question wording on response patterns. *Public Opinion Quarterly* 51: 75–83.

Sniderman, Paul M., and Richard A. Brody. 1977. Coping: The ethic of self-reliance. *American Journal of Political Science* 21: 501–21.

Sniderman, Paul M., and Michael G. Hagen. 1985. *Race and inequality: A study in American values.* Chatham, N.J.: Chatham House Publishers.

Sullivan, John L., James Piereson, and George L. Marcus. 1982. *Political tolerance and American democracy.* Chicago: Univ. of Chicago Press.

Taylor, Shelley E. 1982. The availability bias in social psychology. In Daniel Kahneman, Paul Slovic, and Amos Tversky (eds.), *Judgment under uncertainty: Heuristics and biases.* London: Cambridge Univ. Press.

Taylor, Shelley, E. and Susan T. Fiske. 1979. Salience, attention, and attribution. In Leonard Berkowitz (ed.), *Advances in experimental social psychology,* vol. 11. New York: Academic Press.

Thaler, Richard. 1980. Toward a positive theory of consumer choice. *Journal of Economic Behavior and Organization* 1: 39–60.

References

————. 1987. The psychology and economics conference handbook. In Hillel J. Einhorn and Robin M. Hogarth (eds.), *Rational choice: The contrast between economics and psychology*. Chicago: Univ. of Chicago Press.

Tourangeau, Roger, Kenneth A. Rasinski, and Roy D'Andrade. 1989. Accessibility effects in survey responses. Department of Psychology, Univ. of California, San Diego. Mimeo.

Tuchman, Gaye. 1978. *Making news: A study in the construction of reality.* New York: The Free Press.

U.S. Congress. House. Subcommittee on Public Assistance and Unemployment Compensation. 1985. *Children in Poverty.* 99th Cong., 1st sess., 1985.

Verba, Sidney, and Gary Orren. 1985. *Equality in America: The view from the top.* Cambridge: Harvard Univ. Press.

Walster, Elaine H. 1966. Assignment of responsibility for an accident. *Journal of Personality and Social Psychology* 3: 73–79.

Weaver, Kent R. 1986. The politics of blame avoidance. *Journal of Public Policy* 6: 371–98.

Weaver, Paul H. 1972. Is television news biased? *The Public Interest* 26: 57–74.

Weiner, Bernard. 1985a. "Spontaneous" causal search. *Psychological Bulletin* 97: 74–94.

————. 1985b. An attributional theory of achievement motivation and emotion. *Psychological Review* 92: 548–73.

Weintraub, Bernard. 1985. The presidency: How to blow hot and cold and inspire warmth. *New York Times*, 27 March sec. A.

Weisman, Steven R. 1984. Can the magic prevail? *New York Times Magazine*, 29 April.

Westin, Av. 1982. *Newswatch: How television decides the news.* New York: Simon & Schuster.

Wortman, Camille B. 1976. Causal attributions and personal control. In John H. Harvey, William Ickes, and Robert F. Kidd (eds.), *New directions in attribution research*, vol. 1. Hillsdale, N.J.: Lawrence Erlbaum Associates.

Wyer, Robert S., Jr., and Jon Hartwick. 1980. The role of information retrieval and conditional inference processes in belief formation and change. In Leonard Berkowitz (ed.), *Advances in experimental social psychology*, vol. 13. New York: Academic Press.

Wyer, Robert S., Jr., and Thomas K. Srull. 1984. Category accessibility: Some theoretic and empirical issues concerning the processing of social stimulus information. In E. Tory Higgins, Nicholas A. Kuiper, and Mark P. Zanna (eds.), *Social cognition: The Ontario symposium*. Hillsdale, N.J.: Lawrence Erlbaum Associates.

References

———. 1986. Human cognition in its social context. *Psychological Review* 93: 322–59.

Zaller, John, and Stanley Feldman. 1988. Answering questions versus revealing preferences. Paper delivered at the Fifth Annual Meeting of the Political Methodology Society, Los Angeles, Calif.

Index

(Numbers in italics denote pages on which illustrations or tables appear)